# A FRESH APPROACH TO THE
## NEW TESTAMENT

# A Fresh Approach
## to the
# New Testament

✦✦✦✦✦✦✦✦✦✦✦✦✦✦✦✦✦✦✦✦✦✦✦✦✦✦✦✦✦✦✦✦✦✦✦✦✦✦✦✦✦✦✦✦✦✦

## H. G. G. HERKLOTS

✦✦✦✦✦✦✦✦✦✦✦✦✦✦✦✦✦✦✦✦✦✦✦✦✦✦✦✦✦✦✦✦✦✦✦✦✦✦✦✦✦✦✦✦✦✦

New York      Nashville
**ABINGDON-COKESBURY PRESS**

# A FRESH APPROACH TO THE NEW TESTAMENT

SET UP, PRINTED, AND BOUND BY THE PARTHENON PRESS, AT NASHVILLE, TENNESSEE, UNITED STATES OF AMERICA

*Preface*

THE important word in the title of this book is *Approach*. This is not an introduction to the New Testament in any ordinary sense; all it does is to suggest a fresh means of approach. Nor are its contents original; it is possible, however, that they are presented in a way which will be new to many readers.

I am most grateful to Frederic A. Cockin, Bishop of Bristol, for allowing me to use his translation of the Epistle to the Philippians, which, treasured by all who know it, has been too long out of print.

This book is based on lectures given as University Extension Lectures for the Extramural Board of the University of Sheffield, in the Parish Hall at Wombwell in the spring of 1949 and at the university in the autumn.

# Contents

# Contents

# I

## A Fresh Approach?

A FRESH APPROACH to the New Testament? Is that possible at this date in history? Perhaps not. Yet it is hoped that the approach in this book will prove different from those approaches which are most usual. If it is successful, it will be a very old approach which has been made; for the attempt here is to take the reader through some of the stages by which the New Testament came into being, as if he lived in the age for which it was written.

First, however, it will be useful to consider some other possible approaches to this collection of books—for it is a collection, although its authors wrote, every one of them, from the same point of view and under the compulsion of the same great series of historical events. They wrote with a definite purpose; but they did not know that they were writing Scripture, that they were adding to the Bible. In the following generation whenever "Scripture" was quoted by Christian writers, the word always referred to the Old Testament. The record of a sermon delivered at Corinth around A.D. 140, inaccurately named the Second Epistle of Clement, is the earliest known work which refers explicitly to the New Testament as "Scripture." Gradually, however, a list of authoritative books—called the *canon* from a word meaning a measuring rod—was compiled, stimulated by the need for books to read in church services, and the need to exclude heretical teaching. By the fifth century the list was what you will find in a Bible today.

There had been some borderline cases. The book of Revelation, for example, was not in every early list, nor was the Epistle to the Hebrews. Other books, such as the Shepherd of Hermas, an allegory, and the so-called Epistle of Barnabas, won a fleeting authority. There were yet others, hardly serious candidates for inclusion in the canon, which are of value to historians for understanding the life and temper of the early Church. The New Testament had to win its way for acceptance as Scripture. When this was done, or rather, as it was being done, how did men approach it?

Among the Gospels, that attributed to Matthew came first in esteem. Very quickly it became *the* Gospel. It was always quoted in preference to the others unless the needed sentence could only be found elsewhere. By the latter half of the second century the existence of *four* Gospels was taken for granted. The Christian historian Irenaeus held that the number was four of necessity: "For since there are four regions of the world wherein we are, and four principal winds, and the Church is as seed sown in the whole earth, and the Gospel is the Church's pillar and ground, and the breath of life: it is natural that it should have four pillars, from all quarters

breathing incorruption, and kindling men into life." [1]
This argument is hardly likely to commend itself to
modern people, yet the fact that it was advanced in the
latter half of the second century is evidence that by then
Christians were well accustomed to there being four
Gospels, no more and no less. Their uncanonical competitors were finding their own level as the wonder-
crammed products of a wonder-loving age. Among the
four, Matthew had the pre-eminence, and Mark was
least esteemed. Jerome at the end of the fourth century
regarded Mark as an abridgment of Matthew; and this
was a common belief until the rise of modern scholar-
ship, which sent Mark into the first place as a primary
source used by both Matthew and Luke.

Many early Christians—and many Christians of all
subsequent ages—approached the New Testament
through Matthew. But even in antiquity people were
aware of the difficulties caused by divergent accounts
of the same event. To overcome these the nineteenth
century wrote *Lives of Christ* in which differences were
smoothed out and a choice made between conflicting
narratives. Toward the end of the second century a
much-traveled Syrian from Mesopotamia, named Tatian,
made a similar attempt. His *Diatessaron*—the name
means *By Four*—made a continuous story from the gospel narratives, using the Gospel of John to provide the
outline. Among Syriac-speaking Christians this work was
very popular. Indeed, says Streeter, until about A.D. 430

[1] *Adversus Haereses* III. 11. 8.

the *Diatessaron* provided the only form in which the Gospels were read in their churches or commented upon by their theologians. With them it was the *Diatessaron*, rather than Matthew, which was quoted as *the* Gospel; they used the separate Gospels very little.

Here, then, were two approaches to the New Testament already established by the end of the second century. Early also the method of "allegorical interpretation" was used to explain away difficulties and to fill out teaching. This began with fresh interpretations of the Old Testament, as if God treated "Israel as a sort of picture-gallery in which to hang up from time to time futurist sketches of the life of Jesus, so mistily painted that their subject would remain hopelessly obscure until Christ had come." [2] Not all here was mistaken or wholly to be discarded, for these men realized the essential continuity of the New Israel, the Church, with the earlier People of God. Allegorical interpretation applied to the New Testament could, however, produce ludicrous results. Professor Dodd has recalled what Augustine made of the parable of the good Samaritan—interpreting Jerusalem as the heavenly city of peace, from whose blessedness Adam fell, Jericho as the moon, signifying our mortality, the thieves as the devil and his angels, and so on, until the inn is the Church, the morrow is after the resurrection of the Lord, the two pence the two precepts of love (or the promise of this life and that which is to come), and the innkeeper the apostle Paul.[3]

[2] W. A. L. Elmslie, *How Came Our Faith*, p. 74.
[3] *The Parable of the Kingdom*, pp. 11-12.

If this were indeed the purport of the parable, those who heard it—and, in particular, the lawyer who prompted it by his question, "And who is my neighbour?"—could not have understood its meaning at all. When Saul of Tarsus was converted to the Christian faith, did his instructors tell him that he had already appeared, under the guise of an innkeeper, in one of the Master's best-known parables? Allegorical interpretation may have its uses, but its pitfalls are yawning chasms.

The approach to the New Testament of modern students has usually been different from any of these. An understanding of the synoptic problem[4] has been the indispensable basis of their studies. That the first three Gospels bear some relation to one another is clear to anyone who has read them. Similarities of language, even more convincing in the original Greek than in English, occur not only in the recorded words of Jesus, but in the descriptions of his actions. It is natural, perhaps, that Matthew, Mark, and Luke should each quote the words of Jesus, in roughly identical form, in the account of the healing of a paralytic at Capernaum. These words would be treasured. But an explanatory clause, awkwardly placed, would hardly be transmitted orally. Yet Matt. 9:6 reads: "But that ye may know that the Son of man hath power on earth to forgive sins (*then saith he to the sick of the palsy*), Arise." [5] Mark

[4] The first three Gospels are often called the Synoptic Gospels. The synoptic problem is concerned with their relationship to each other.

[5] Unless otherwise indicated all scriptural quotations are from the Revised Version of 1881-85.

2:10-11 has similarly: "But that ye may know that the Son of man hath power on earth to forgive sins (*he saith to the sick of the palsy*), I say unto thee, Arise." Luke 5:24 is very little different: "But that ye may know that the Son of man hath power on earth to forgive sins (*he said unto him that was palsied*), I say unto thee, Arise." The placing of the awkward clause in parentheses, over which readers in church have stumbled for more than eighteen centuries, makes it clear that somebody did some copying.

The work of nineteenth- and twentieth-century scholars has established almost beyond cavil that Mark was the earliest-written Gospel, used by the authors of both Matthew and Luke, though used in a different way; that Matthew and Luke had another written source, or sources, before them, composed in the main of records of the teaching of Jesus, which it has been customary to call Q, from the German *Quelle,* a source. More recently it has been emphasized that both Matthew and Luke had their own written sources which they regarded as being quite as important as Mark or Q. For the ordinary student approaching the New Testament the consequence of all this detailed scholarly knowledge has been that the approach to the New Testament has been through Mark, or through a consideration of the three Synoptic Gospels set out in parallel columns. One group of students who did this had a limited time at their disposal but were fascinated by the intricacies of the documentary relationship of the Gospels. Later they considered as much of the actual Gospels as they had time for; but they never reached beyond the Galilean ministry and so failed, in that course at any rate, really to discover what the books which they were discussing were about. The Cross and Resurrection come in the later chapters of the Gospels. But for their writers they provided the starting point, the reason for their writing at all. It may still be right for most people to start with Mark, but those who do so had best begin their study by reading that short Gospel right through.

The first readers of the New Testament were not students of the synoptic problem. They did not even begin with Mark. It is much more likely that—to their consternation as well as ours—they began with Galatians. The key to the understanding of the New Testament documents is that they are the *propagandist literature of a widespread and successful missionary movement.* This is a forgotten platitude. The instructed schoolboy knows that Paul of Tarsus went on missionary journeys; he may even be able to make an outline of these upon a map. But it has been too little realized that these were not the only missionary journeys which were taking place. In the forties and fifties of the first century the Christian message was spreading with great rapidity round the eastern end of the Mediterranean. The eighteenth chapter of Acts, which records events which took place at Corinth around A.D. 51-53, tells how Priscilla and Aquila arrived there from Rome—and they were already Christians. Apollos came from Alexandria, and he also had been partially instructed in the Christian faith. Read the epistles of Paul and notice the number of his associates mentioned by name, with some title added to indicate their missionary experience; they are his fellow workers, fellow prisoners, fellow slaves. "If we were to mark on the map the routes of all their journeys which are known to us, the lines would almost make a labyrinth, but we should feel all the more clearly how the Anatolian world was set thrilling by the trumpet blasts of the evangelists." [6] When persecution arose under Nero in A.D. 64, the most powerful police state in the world found itself impotent to prevent the spread of this puzzling faith.[7]

If we are to understand a missionary movement—in the past or present, Moslem, Communist, or Christian—there are certain questions which must be asked.

1. We need to know something about the missionaries themselves. What is their background? What experience has led them to the hazardous task of persuading other people—perhaps alien in race, culture, or language—that what they have to say is true? Why do they believe that it is a matter of life and death that others should accept their message?

2. We must have some understanding of the actual message which they are trying to communicate.

3. We must know something of the circumstances of the time and of the rival faiths in the field.

4. If the mission is successful, we must try to discover the factors, in the message itself, in the life which it pro-

---

[6] Adolf Deissmann, *Paul, A Study in Social and Religious History* (2nd ed. 1926), p. 241.

[7] Dom Gregory Dix in a lecture to the Sheffield Theological Society.

duces, and in the circumstances of the time, which contributed to that success.

It is to these questions that we must address ourselves if we are to make a right approach to the missionary literature which we call the New Testament.

# II

## The Missionaries

WHAT do we know about the missionaries themselves? A great deal in general but, with the notable exception of Paul of Tarsus, not very much
in particular. In the first place they were Jews, disciples
of Jesus of Nazareth, to whom they gave the title of
Christ or Messiah. No one seriously supposed that they
had only themselves to talk about. This was recognized
by their opponents. When the Jewish hierarchy was astonished by the uprising of what they could only regard
as a heretical sect, they quickly realized that Jesus of
Nazareth, whom they had thought to be safely dead and
buried, lay behind it all. "Now when they saw the boldness of Peter and John, and perceived that they were un-
learned, ordinary laymen, they marvelled; and they
recognized them as having been with Jesus." (Acts
4:13.) [1]

Their Gentile opponents were to arrive at the same
conclusion. When the cultured Roman aristocrat Tacitus came to describe the great fire of Rome in A.D. 64, he
told how the blame for it was shifted onto the Chris-

---

[1] The translation is that of *The Book of Books*.

tians. Because nothing could dispel the suspicion that
the fire had broken out by order of the emperor,

Nero set up as culprits and punished with the utmost
refinement of cruelty a class hated for their abominations,
who are commonly called Christians. Christus, from whom
their name is derived, was executed at the hands of the procurator Pontius Pilate in the reign of Tiberius. Checked for
the moment, this pernicious superstition again broke out,
not only in Judaea, the source of the evil, but even in Rome,
that receptacle for everything that is sordid and degrading
from every quarter of the globe, which there finds a following.[2]

Tacitus had not a very elevated view of Christianity,
but he knew that it was to be traced to Judea, to one
who bore the name of Christ. More than this, he had
stated one phrase in the Church's creed, "Suffered under
Pontius Pilate."

The same claim was, of course, made by the Christian
missionaries themselves. The supercilious Athenian
crowd, listening to Paul as he vainly tried to meet them
on their own level, concluded that he was "a setter
forth of strange gods: because he preached Jesus and the
resurrection" (Acts 17:18) —perhaps thinking that the
Greek word for resurrection, *anastasis,* which the speaker
linked so often with the name of Jesus, was the title of
a goddess! His own claim, when set down in writing, was
clear enough. Christian preachers are Christian
preachers only when they can say, "We preach not our-

[2] *Annales* XV.44.

selves, but Christ Jesus as Lord, and ourselves as your servants for Jesus' sake" (II Cor. 4:5) .

The first Christian missionaries, then, were Jews who had been disciples of Jesus of Nazareth, who had become his apostles, or messengers, but who remained his disciples, or learners, always. They were Jews who thought in Jewish categories. Their native language was Aramaic, the Syrian tongue which had displaced Hebrew except for religious purposes. In the end, however, their message was to be rejected by Judaism and accepted by the Greek culture to which they felt in many ways so alien. After the fall of Jerusalem in A.D. 70 it became clear that Christianity was decisively rejected by the Jewish synagogues. It persisted because it was sufficiently adaptable to reclothe itself in a Greek dress. From our present point of view, however, all this lay in the future. The first Christian missionaries were Jews. It was in the synagogue that they had been brought up; it was to the synagogue that they went with their new message.

Because they had been schooled in the synagogue they were far from being uneducated. W. A. Curtis said:

If we speak of Galilean or Judaean "peasants," we are by no means at liberty to associate illiteracy or ignorance with the name. Indeed the only other nations which have ever rivalled the Israel of the ancient Synagogue in respect of their high level of educated intelligence have been those which at the Reformation followed the Jewish example and made education, based on the Scriptures, both a national and a spiritual possession for man and woman and child.[3]

[3] *Jesus Christ the Teacher,* p. 23.

Before Jesus called them, they knew their Scriptures well; it was not their teachers' fault if they did not know many passages of them by heart; and if Jesus interpreted those Scriptures in a way which astonished them, they knew well enough what he was talking about. Their view of God was not vague. It was definite, for they were heirs to the teaching of the prophets. Their inheritance, reinterpreted by Jesus, is the inheritance also of the Christian Church; it is one of its indispensable foundations. A. P. Stanley displayed a right sense of proportion, though he may have flouted convenience, when upon his appointment as regius professor of ecclesiastical history at Oxford at the close of 1856, he began his lectures with Abraham.

The emergence of the prophets in the little states of Israel and Judah is one of the most remarkable events in the history of the world. The philosopher A. N. Whitehead wrote: "Our civilization owes to them more than we can express. They constitute one of the few groups of men who decisively altered history in any intimate sense." [4] The prophetic teachings had indeed been overlaid by much subsequent interpretation in the Judaism of the time of Jesus; but the prophetic view of God—so different from any view of God held by any other people —was still maintained. The very law books which the religious teachers regarded as of prime importance were in part an attempt to reduce to a practicable code the ideals which the prophets had proclaimed.

For the Jews, God was Creator. The first Hebrew

[4] *Adventures of Ideas*, p. 62.

sentence which the modern student learns—*Bereshith bara Elohim eth ha shamaim we'eth ha aretz,* "In the beginning God created the heaven and the earth"—was also the first sentence which the Christian missionaries had learned when they went as boys to the elementary school at the local synagogue. The belief that God made the world is a foundation for morality and a spur to effort. If you hold the cyclical view of history—as did so many of the peoples of antiquity—believing that time goes round and round, that at some moment in the distant future you will be once again in the same place as you are now, reading this book, with the same personal problems to face, and the same fears for the future of the world; if you really believe this, you will know that nothing you can do will ever be of any avail. Or should you hold, with Lucretius and Bertrand Russell, that the universe is an accident, the result of a fortuitous concatenation of atoms, you will not easily find convincing reasons for moral effort. You will make the best of it, no doubt, but nothing more. It is those who believe that God made the world who can be forward-looking. They may believe, as do Christians, that the world has been marred by man's rebellion. But Christians, as we shall see, believe also that God himself has come to the aid of man in his distress, summoning him to a share in the rescue work of the Second Adam.

There was nothing capricious in the God whom the Jews worshiped. He was *law*. Elijah taunted the prophets of Baal: "Cry aloud: for he is a god; either he is musing, or he is gone aside, or he is in a journey, or peradventure he sleepeth and must be awakened" (I Kings 18:27). It was a biting taunt, for the prophets of Baal really did believe that their god might be so occupied; their very sacrifices were a kind of bribe to secure his attention. Hebrew religion arose in part from similar beliefs, but through the prophets it came to believe in a transcendent God, wholly self-consistent. "Hast thou not known? hast thou not heard? the everlasting God, the Lord, the Creator of the ends of the earth, fainteth not, neither is weary: there is no searching of his understanding." (Isa. 40:28.) Yet this great God was not the irresponsible despot of Islam. He was reliable. The agreements he had made with his people would, on his side, be scrupulously kept. The historical books of the Old Testament recorded his dealings with men; because in doing so they revealed his nature, they were placed by the Hebrews in the roll of the prophets. Here we see how God respected the particular people with whom he had entered into a covenant relationship. Just because that relationship was not make-believe, for men to break it was the prelude to disaster. "Just because you are the only nation in the world with whom I have come into close relation, I will punish you for all your crimes." (Amos 3:2.) [5]

God, in consequence, was the *Lord of history*. Though he had entered into a special relation with one nation, he was concerned with every nation. He could use Assyria as the rod of his anger (Isa. 10:5). Israel was

[5] T. H. Robinson, tr., *Books of the Old Testament in Colloquial Speech.*

never to pride itself upon being a chosen people. "Do you realize that I think of you Israelites just as I think of African negroes? It is true that I brought up Israel from Egypt, but it is equally true that I was responsible for the coming of the Philistines from Crete and of the Syrians from Kir." (Amos 9:7, Robinson tr.) On June 6, 1944, famous as D-Day, Archbishop Temple gave a lecture on Christianity as an interpretation of history. He quoted the closing verses of Isa. 19, when the prophet, addressing people who are near to being crushed between the mighty armies of Assyria and Egypt, says (vss. 23-25):

In that day shall there be a highway out of Egypt to Assyria, and the Assyrian shall come into Egypt, and the Egyptian into Assyria, and the Egyptians shall worship with the Assyrians. In that day shall Israel be the third with Egypt and with Assyria, a blessing in the midst of the earth; for that the Lord of hosts hath blessed them saying Blessed be Egypt my people and Assyria the work of my hands and Israel mine inheritance.

The Archbishop added:

It is as if you were to say, "In that day shall Britain be the third, with Germany and Japan, even a blessing in the midst of the earth: whom the Lord of hosts shall bless, saying Blessed be Germany my people and Japan the work of mine hands and Britain mine inheritance." [6]

The Hebrews looked forward. Events were not predetermined and recurrent, held by the remorseless wheel of fate. Nor did these men constantly look back to a

[6] *Christianity as an Interpretation of History,* p. 17.

Golden Age in the past. If they looked back to the Garden of Eden, it was to a time when things went grievously wrong, which yet held promise for the future (cf. Gen. 3:14-19). If they looked back to their deliverance from Egypt, it was to recall the ceaseless fidelity of their God. For many centuries they looked forward to a good time that was coming. As early as the eighth century B.C. Amos told the Israelites that the Day of the Lord, which they anticipated with such eagerness, would be one of judgment upon their sin, a day of darkness rather than of light (5:18). Gradually this hope crystallized around a looked-for future figure, the Messiah, or anointed one. He would be a leader sent by God, revealing his will, vindicating his moral character. Yet the purpose of his coming the Israelites were in danger of forgetting. They came to think of him as *their* avenger, as the captain victorious over *their* enemies, as the bringer-in of a period of postwar prosperity when hard-working prisoners of war would minister to *their* comforts. During the Exile, it is true, a prophet had spoken of one "despised and rejected of men; a man of sorrows and acquainted with grief, and as one from whom men hide their face" (Isa. 53:3). No ordinary Jew accepted this as a portrait of the Messiah. For him the Suffering Servant was Israel. The Jewish Targum or paraphrase of Isa. 53 does indeed identify the Servant with the Messiah, but "diverts the element of humiliation, suffering, and death from the person of the Servant-Messiah and transfers it to Israel or to the heathen nations." [7]

[7] William Manson, *Jesus the Messiah*, p. 168. Dr. Manson prints sections of the Targum alongside the biblical verses to which they refer.

Many modern men regard religion as little more than doing good; fundamentally they agree with Matthew Arnold's definition that it is "morality touched with emotion." This definition is wholly inadequate, but it contains an important element which we owe to the prophets. Ancient religion was little concerned with morality; Greek philosophers looked down upon the degraded morality implicit in the religious myths upon which they had been brought up. Religion was a means of getting on the good side of unseen forces. "The Alpha and Omega of a pagan's religious action and prayer is 'My will be done,' and when his request is not fulfilled, his religion has failed him." [8] This was as true of the official religions of Greece and Rome as those of the African bush. But the Hebrew prophets taught that a good God could not be worshiped in ways that were impure. A righteous God demanded righteous dealings between men. "You must aim at good and not evil if you would save your lives, and if Yahweh the God of Hosts is to be with you, as you say he is. You must hate evil and love goodness. You must see that real justice has its place in the law courts." (Amos 5:14-15, Robinson tr.) This teaching is summarized in Mic. 6:8: "He hath shewed thee, O man, what is good; and what doth the Lord require of thee, but to do justly, and to love mercy, and to walk humbly with thy God." The conception of walking meant much to the Jews, as it did to the early Church; it implied the ordinary duties of everyday life.

---

[8] Diedrich Westermann, *Africa and Christianity*, p. 75.

Jews and Christians were alone in thinking that these could be performed in God's company.

In the synagogues where the first Christian missionaries were educated the Law held pride of place. This contained the first five books of our Bible, traditionally associated with Moses. Deuteronomy was, however, an end product of the teachings of the eighth-century prophets; much of the rest had been rewritten during the Exile in Babylon in the sixth century or later. An attempt, heroic if impossible, was thus made to turn principles into rules governing practice. "Pharisaism and Deuteronomy," it has been said, "came into the world the same day." [9] Law, for us, has a forbidding sound; what it could mean to a Jew is to be discovered from the incessant repetitions of Ps. 119:

O take not the word of thy truth utterly out of my mouth:
  for my hope is in thy judgments.
So shall I alway keep thy law: yea, for ever and ever.
And I will walk at liberty: for I seek thy commandments.
(Vss. 43-45.) [10]

For a Hebrew the Law meant a way of life which distinguished him from all other men and made him what he was. Jesus of Nazareth also was educated in the synagogue. The Law provided his summary of the commandments; quotations from Deuteronomy were often on his lips.

[9] John Skinner, *Prophecy and Religion*, p. 96.
[10] *Book of Common Prayer* (Church of England) translation.

27

Law requires interpretation; interpretation of law breeds lawyers. In the Palestine of the first century the religious lawyers—the scribes—were many; they interpreted the books of Moses and reinterpreted the interpretations of others. Those who have dealt with a modern government department can form some conception of the finesse which these interpretations required and the tiny details to which they extended. Many of the scribes belonged to the Pharisaic party. The Pharisees were those who took their religion very seriously. They were enthusiasts for the Law, and their lives echoed the piety of Ps. 119. In the temple, however, an opposition party, the Sadducees, was in charge, much more ready to compromise with modern ideas and foreign ways of life. The influence of the Pharisees was dominant in the synagogues of the land—which were something like a church on the Sabbath, but more like a school for the rest of the week—and in many of those which had sprung up where the Jews were scattered abroad. In the end all the parties in Palestine rejected the claims of Jesus of Nazareth and combined with the Romans to encompass his execution. The best religion which the world had known, and the best form of law, the Roman, united to bring this about.

Christianity did not arise by some inevitable evolution from Judaism. If evolutionary language is used, it might be described as a mutation. To the Jews its claims were scandalous; every possible effort must be made to suppress them. So thought one who became the greatest Christian missionary. Saul of Tarsus was so impressed by the new menace that he "went unto the high priest, and asked of him letters to Damascus unto the synagogues, that if he found any that were of the Way, whether men or women, he might bring them bound to Jerusalem" (Acts 9:1-2). Already he had seen the first Christian martyr, Stephen, done to death. Perhaps he had been impressed by the manner in which this able man met his death, praying for his persecutors, a manner reminiscent of Jesus of Nazareth. Yet the fact that the followers of this new faith possessed the power of impressing even such a man as Saul made him redouble his efforts for its suppression. They were proclaiming the direst blasphemy, that the Messiah had come, that he had been rejected and suffered the utter humiliation of death upon a cross at Gentile hands. Did not the Law itself declare: "He that is hanged is accursed of God" (Deut. 21:23)? Yet the tension developing in his mind prepared him for the miracle of the Damascus road, when his life was revolutionized by what he ever held to be the personal intervention of the living Christ. The prayer of Stephen for one of his persecutors had been answered.

In time this man became the great missionary, exponent, and defender of the faith whose adherents he had once oppressed. In the past he had tried to keep all the ritual requirements of the Jewish Law; he had found the task impossible and the attempt unsatisfying. Now he walked in freedom, knowing that his worthlessness had been counted worthy by Jesus Christ. A curse indeed lay upon the one whom they hanged upon a tree, but it was the curse of man's sin borne freely by one in whom dwelt all the fullness of the Godhead bodily. The Jews remained a privileged people, but their privileges were surrendered unless they accepted the new privilege of serving Christ and making him known to all men. The old Israel had proved unworthy, but a new Israel had now arisen in which former aliens had become fellow citizens with those Jews who had acknowledged their Messiah. The new Israel was heir to all the promises made to the old, and language descriptive of the old was reminted to describe the astonishing phenomenon of the new. Peter raided Deuteronomy and Isaiah, Exodus, Hosea, and the Psalms to make a description of the new People of God:

> But ye are an elect race, a royal priesthood, a holy nation, a people for God's own possession, that ye may shew forth the excellencies of him who called you out of darkness into his marvellous light: which in time past were no people, but now are the people of God: which had not obtained mercy, but now have obtained mercy. (I Pet. 2:9-10.)

The creation of this people was the consequence of the missionary preaching, but earlier still it was the consequence of the act of God in Christ by which the missionaries themselves had been brought out of darkness into his marvelous light. Simon Peter could never forget the crowning mercy of his own forgiveness. Saul of Tarsus could write of "the son of God, who loved me, and gave himself up for me." This is the spring of missionary endeavor in every age.

# III

## The Mission Field

THERE is no more common complaint of modern life than that it is all very complicated. Newspapers sweep us from crisis to crisis, whose origins are distant and obscure, whose significance eludes the comprehension of ordinary people and divides the experts into antagonistic camps. A century from now it may prove possible to sort it out, to discover the really significant trends; at present this certainty is denied us,

> And we are here as on a darkling plain
> Swept with confused alarms of struggle and flight,
> Where ignorant armies clash by night.

Our successors may be able to make generalizations about the twentieth century as we today can make them about the nineteenth, which Matthew Arnold found so disturbing. While we endeavor to keep our heads, and to follow those who seem to be ahead of us, it is encouraging to realize that this is not the first age which has recognized itself as complicated. Few ages have deserved the epithet more than that in which the Christian message was first proclaimed, but we can now discover some of the significant trends in its life and organize them in a pattern which contemporaries could not discern. The business of a historian, said Lucian, is to superinduce upon events the charm of order. It is only upon charts extending over centuries, and maps equally large, that this order begins to be discernible.

It was part of the greatness of Paul of Tarsus that he was ahead of his time, that he could see the developing pattern of God's purpose and set it out majestically:

This Secret was hidden to past generations of mankind, but it has now, by the Spirit, been made plain to God's consecrated Messengers and Prophets. It is simply this: that the Gentiles, who were previously excluded from God's Agreements, are to be equal heirs with His chosen people, equal members and equal partners in God's Promise given by Christ through the Gospel. (Eph. 3:5-6.) [1]

Yet how complicated a figure was this Paul. (Every reader knows that he could be addressed by two different names.) Put one question to him and how does he answer? He can count up his Jewish qualifications on the fingers of his hands:

*circumcised the eighth day* (which was as it should be),
*of the stock of Israel,*
*of the tribe of Benjamin* (prestige is here being claimed; it was the best tribe to belong to!),
*a Hebrew of Hebrews* (i.e., a Hebrew son of Hebrew parents);
*as touching the law, a Pharisee;*

[1] J. B. Phillips, *Letters to Young Churches.* Copyright 1947 by the Macmillan Co., and used by their permission.

*as touching zeal, persecuting the church;*
*as touching the righteousness which is in the law, found*
*blameless.* (Phil. 3:5-6.)

Put another question to Paul—or rather, forget to put another question—and his statement is different:

They have beaten us publicly, uncondemned, *men that are Romans,* and cast us into prison; and do they now cast us out privily? nay verily; but let them come themselves and bring us out. And the lictors reported these words unto the praetors: and they feared, when they heard that they were Romans. (Acts 16:37-38.)

Another time he could recall his birthplace with pride:

I am a Jew, of Tarsus in Cilicia, a citizen of no mean city. (Acts 21:39.)

A rabbinically-trained Jew who was also a Roman citizen, he was also a Greek-speaking man from Asia Minor. Even when he wrote to the church in Rome it was in Greek, not in Latin. His mastery of the language led Gilbert Murray to say that he is "certainly one of the greatest figures in Greek literature."

This kind of complication is to be found not only in the Acts and in the epistles, but in the Gospels. One of the most searching questions put to Jesus of Nazareth involved someone's running out of the temple courts to fetch him a Roman denarius. The burden of taxation in Palestine, with two taxing authorities, one religious and the other civil, each disregarding the other, was almost more than people could bear; there were many good reasons for tax gatherers to be unpopular in Palestine. Galilee in the time of Jesus was governed as a native state under the Roman Empire by the not-so-native Herod Antipas, whose family came from across the Dead Sea. Judea, on the other hand, was ruled directly by Pontius Pilate, one of the Roman procurators who had been put there, at the inhabitants' own request, in place of the bloodthirsty Archelaus, the worst of the sons of Herod the Great. Greek, Roman, and Hebrew influences interpenetrate the background in which the mission of Jesus was set. Roman centurions are among the attractive figures in the story. Jesus would not have to travel far from Nazareth to find a Greek temple; they were there in Decapolis. The word Galilee itself, meaning district, was shortened from Galilee of the Gentiles; much of the mission of Jesus took place in lands which had been recaptured from heathenism. When he went outside his own country, traveling farther north, he probably talked to the Syrophenician woman in Greek (Mark 7:26). At least some of his first disciples were bilingual. When "certain Greeks among those that went up to worship at the feast" wanted to see Jesus, they sought out "Philip, which was of Bethsaida of Galilee" (John 12:21), a largely foreign town whose inhabitants probably spoke more Greek than Aramaic.

Thus the complicated stage was set for a drama which was to culminate in a cross, over which a name would be written "in Hebrew, and in Latin, and in Greek" (John 19:20). For that culmination all the cultural forces of the world around the Mediterranean had prepared.

When it was reached, history had a new beginning. This neither the procurator, nor the religious leaders, nor the mob discerned, but there was a centurion who may have had some inkling of it.

To understand this setting it is necessary to go back more than three hundred years before the Christian Era. The Greek which Paul of Tarsus was to write had received its most perfect literary expression when Greece was a congeries of small city states. No state should be so large, it was held, that all its citizens could not hear the voice of a single herald. Today, in a way undreamed of by the Greeks, this has become possible through broadcasting. In the fourth century B.C., however, Philip, ruler of Macedonia to the north of Greece proper, created a strong army and brought these states together in a loose union. His son, Alexander, succeeded to his position in 336 B.C. and at once determined to attack Persia, the ancient enemy. There followed one of the most remarkable series of military exploits in history. Alexander did what he set out to do, and more. His disciplined troops defeated Darius and took Greek language and culture outside known geography. The crocodiles in the Indus made him think that he had reached the headwaters of the Nile. Where he went he founded cities. Alexander was more dominated by the past than he knew; what he founded were in essence Greek city states. There were many Alexandrias; the most famous of them gave Egypt a port and created a center of Greek culture where even the Jews demanded that the Old Testament should be in Greek. Kandahar

*35*

also bears his name; and Secunderabad, situated where Alexander thought that there was only ocean, is a tribute to his legend.

Greek ideas had indeed been spreading into Asia for a considerable time. When Alexander fought Darius, there were more real Greeks in the army of the Persian monarch than in that of the Macedonian invader. Greek colonization in Asia Minor was not new. Yet Alexander's empire was without precedent. There was no color bar between Greeks and Persians—there was no real color difference—and, as always, matrimony followed the flag. On one occasion Alexander gave dowries to ten thousand of his troops who had married in Asia. The complaint soon circulated that Alexander had himself become orientalized. He could not rise above the flattery which the Persians had given their own monarchs and which they gave as readily to him. If they called him divine, had not his own tutor, Aristotle, spoken of the godlike man who was above human laws? Typical of Alexander, and typical of the new Hellenistic age[2] which his conquests initiated, was the copy of Homer's *Iliad* which he took with him wherever he went, in a jeweled casket, the spoil of an early Syrian victory.

The cultural influence of these conquests is understood when it is remembered that settlers followed the army.

[2] The earlier Greek civilization is called Hellenic. Hellenistic is the word used to describe the diluted Greek culture spread widely in the lands which had formed part of Alexander's empire.

For once the way into Persia was opened, thither for several generations streamed the surplus population of the Aegean Archipelago and its environs. . . . And once they were committed to movement in that direction, they could not draw back. No matter what happened in the West they had yet to Hellenize the world in which the Macedonian had made them masters or themselves go under. Hellenism failed to master the intractable soil of the Orient; but it acquired a capacity for world-culture in the attempt. What led the proud Roman conqueror captive was not the aristocratic civilization of Attic Greece, but the more seductive, accommodating, catholic modification of it which we call Hellenistic.[3]

The early Christian missionaries traveled through the Roman Empire. In Western Europe, Rome put its own stamp upon lands which had previously been barbarous; but in the East the Romans, conscious that they were moving among peoples who were in many ways their cultural superiors, accepted the stamp which Alexander had made. "When Greece had been enslaved, she made a slave of her rough conqueror, and introduced the arts into Latium while it was still uncultured." So wrote the Roman poet Horace, while Juvenal complained that the Syrian Orontes flowed into the Tiber. It was part of a general current, social and religious, flowing from East to West.

The task was too great even for Alexander. His new domains in Asia drained away the best from Greece, so that, when the time came, it was no match for Rome. He was only thirty-two when he died, and his death pro-

[3] W. S. Ferguson in *Cambridge Ancient History*, vol. II, ch. 1.

duced civil war on an imperial scale. Yet he had given a
second language to the whole Near Eastern world. The
Koine, or common Greek, in which a man might make
himself understood from Mersa Matruh to Samarkand,
was the language in which—though with a noticeably
Hebrew accent, and with Hebrew allusions that were
caviar to the general—the New Testament was written.
Discoveries of papyri from this period—personal letters,
legal documents, and bills written on paper made from
the pith of Nile reeds—preserved in the dry sands of
Egypt have served greatly to increase our knowledge of
the New Testament. The spread of this language meant
that "men of culture everywhere, irrespective of race,
had one further element and agency of exchange in
common—a fact which political thinking could not over-
look." [4] The Koine thus played a part similar to that
played in India by the English language, which, since
Macaulay's momentous decision in 1835, became the
basis of higher education throughout the country and
proved to be one of the most influential factors giving
coherence to the political aspirations of its diverse
peoples.

The Greek settlers who followed in Alexander's tracks
took their gods with them, yet they were quite ready to
equate them with the gods they found. There is only
one instance in the records of Christian missionaries
being confronted with a language problem—at Lystra,
in the highlands of Anatolia beyond the Taurus Mountains. Paul had cured a cripple, and immediately the

[4] *Ibid.,* p. 37.

people began to shout out in the local language that the gods had come down in the likeness of men. Soon Paul discovered, to his mingled horror and embarrassment, that the priest of Zeus had arrived, with garlanded oxen which he proposed to sacrifice before them. Here is an illustration of superficial Hellenization. "They called Barnabas, Zeus; and Paul, Hermes, because he was the chief speaker." (Acts 14:12.) Zeus and Hermes were Greek names which had been attached to the local gods. An old-established fertility cult was given a pseudo-Greek respectability in an area where Greek was far from being the first language. And the English translators have taken their cue from the people of Lystra by substituting for the Greek names Zeus and Hermes their Latin equivalents, Jupiter and Mercury.

Paul was proud to be a citizen of the Roman Empire, which had brought peace and order to so large an area of Europe, Asia, and North Africa. Its boundaries were the Atlantic and the Rhine, the Danube and the Euphrates. Within this area there was disarmament—except for the imperial forces—and comparatively free trade. Travel also was frequent. Professional men tended to be migratory; there were many traveling teachers; there were traveling merchants and craftsmen. The imperial forces were cosmopolitan in membership—and they might be sent to serve a thousand miles away at short notice. A military cemetery in Mainz shows that the men buried there came from the Rhine, Holland, Brabant, Hungary, Carinthia, Styria, the Tyrol, Dalmatia, Rumelia, Syria, Spain, France, and Italy. There were probably far fewer restrictions upon travel in Eastern Europe than there are today, though an entertaining story from one of the books of the apocryphal New Testament goes to show that the traveler had to face discomforts which have persisted through the centuries. The Acts of John tells how the apostle and his disciples made themselves at home for the night in a deserted inn. He found the bed infested with bugs, whom he addressed as follows: "I say unto you, O bugs, behave yourselves, one and all, and leave your abode for this night and remain quiet in one place, and keep your distance from the servants of God." On the next morning, when the disciples opened the door, "[they] saw at the door of the house which [they] had taken a great number of bugs standing." These were now addressed a second time by John: "Since ye have well behaved yourselves in hearkening to my rebuke, come unto your place." Whereupon they "running from the door hasted to the bed and climbed up by the legs thereof and disappeared into the joints." [5]

Despite the hazards of travel there was a great deal of it. Most of the better pottery found upon Roman sites in Britain was made in Southern France. Three busts made of Italian marble were recently discovered at a Roman villa excavated at Lullingstone in Kent. Town life tended to have similar features from one side of the empire to the other, as it has today from coast to coast of the United States. Soldiers recruited in Anatolia took Mithraism[6] with them to Hadrian's Wall. The same ease

[5] M. R. James, tr., *The Apocryphal New Testament*, pp. 242-43.

[6] See below, p. 45.

of communication made possible the rapid spread of the Christian faith.

In this world also, physical uprooting, new experiences, and new disappointments brought about a widespread sense of frustration, emptiness, and fear. In the Greek city state the artist or writer had been responsible to an immediate public whose judgment he respected. In the larger Hellenistic world there was no such immediate public; authors who tried to write for mankind wrote in the end only for themselves. Cultural leadership was in the hands of irresponsible *déracinés*. Religion could only be a dying force when men addressed their god as " 'Thou of many names' or by all the names strung together which each worshipper happened to know, accepting as valid every local mode of divine approach when it was not too repellent." [7] Individualism brought its nemesis in the feeling that there was nowhere that a man belonged.

This is one of those shiftings of mood which come in the life of peoples as well as in that of individuals, hard to account for, except partially, hard often to grasp with any precision. A feeling came over men, and suddenly the familiar universe seemed a strange place, terrifying in its enormous magnitude—the earth stretching into regions of unexplored possibilities, moved and shaken by inhuman forces, and over all the silent enigma of the wheeling stars. They awoke, as it were, to find themselves lost in the streets of a huge, strange city.[8]

[7] Ferguson, *op. cit.,* p. 5.
[8] Edwyn Bevan, *Stoics and Sceptics,* p. 97.

# IV

## Rival Faiths

FOUR competitors endeavored to meet this sense of frustration. The first was *magic*. When many people believe nothing, there are always many other people who believe almost anything. The United States of America presents many parallels to the Hellenistic age. It is interesting to read in the work of an American anthropologist: "It is estimated—I do not know by whom—that the yearly income of the fortunetellers in the United States is a hundred and fifty million dollars." [1] The second competitor was to be found in the *mystery religions* which were pressing into Europe from Egypt and the East. The third was *philosophy,* and in particular Stoicism. The fourth competitor was *Judaism*.

Magic must be distinguished from religion, though the two are often confused.

In magic we do not trust the unseen powers we are dealing with; in religion we do. Bargaining with the gods is not magic, for we cannot bargain even with men unless we have some trust in them. We are not using magic till we endeavour to outwit or wheedle the unseen powers, or to com-

[1] William Howells, *The Heathens*, p. 13.

pel them by the terror of some power supposed to be greater than theirs.[2]

Throughout the Hellenistic period, until the third and fourth centuries A.D., there was a growing appetite for the miraculous and an increasing use of magical formulas.

Many magic papyri are known, with formulae and ceremonies for every sort of personal advantage; they will give success in love or money-making, cure diseases, exorcize devils, destroy an enemy; among them are omnibus charms, good for any purpose. All sorts of materials were in vogue, from the humble onion to the formula, probably seldom used, which begins, "Take an emerald of great price and thereon carve a beetle." [3]

Magicians could hardly have commanded widespread support for so long had they not been able to demonstrate their skill in uncanny ways. They were able somehow to supply what the public continued to demand.[4] Christian apologists in the second century made sparing use of the miracles of Jesus for evidential purposes; their opponents readily admitted these miracles—and ascribed them to magic. What is surprising in the canonical Gospels is the rarity rather than the abundance of the miracles which they record. Miracles are two for a penny in those second-century religious romances which styled

[2] H. M. Gwatkin, *The Knowledge of God and Its Historical Development,* I, 249.

[3] W. W. Tarn, *Hellenistic Civilisation* (2nd ed. 1930) , p. 317.

[4] Cf. H. M. Gwatkin, *Early Church History,* I, 192-93.

themselves gospels. These were typical of the age; they represent what the Church had to struggle against even within its own membership. "He saved others; himself he cannot save." That is what the natural man found so hard to accept, the Christ who did not come down from the cross, but remained there for the world's salvation.

All that magic could offer, all that it has ever offered—from the soothsayers of Babylon to the soothsayers of the modern day—is a box of tricks. As Second Isaiah so clearly realized, it denied the righteousness of God and his orderly government of the universe. What are known as the mystery religions—the religions of Isis and Attis, of Mithras and Serapis, and of many another—which were pressing into Europe endued with the glamour of the enigmatic East offered far more. Indeed what they offered seemed, on the face of it, surprisingly like Christianity—so much so that early Christian writers described their rites as satanic parodies of the Christian sacraments, while some modern writers have concluded that Christianity was itself little more than a mystery religion, the one which somehow happened to possess some survival value. The emotional warmth of some of these rites had a particular attraction for women, who were enjoying a new freedom. Mithraism, on the other hand, was the soldiers' faith; the remains of its altars have been found in military stations from the Solway to the Euphrates. There was much skepticism in the age, which could express itself in the epitaph, "N. F., F., N.S., N.C."—*I was not, I was, I am not, I couldn't care less*. But, as Professor Halliday pointed out, this bravado betrays an uneasiness of soul.[5] Men and women were afraid—afraid of the unknown. The Epistle to the Hebrews hit the nail on the head when it spoke of delivering "all them who through fear of death were all their lifetime subject to bondage" (2:15).

This was exactly what the mystery religions sought to do. They promised salvation—the word was in common use. They spoke of beings whom they addressed as Saviour and Lord. The initiate who had been baptized in the bull's blood of Mithraism was given a mark on his forehead and described as "reborn into eternity." One sect even took an oath at baptism: "I call these seven witnesses to witness that I will sin no more, I will commit adultery no more, I will not steal, I will not act unjustly, I will not covet, I will not hate, I will not despise, nor will I have pleasure in any evil." [6] Mithraism had a communion service in memory of the last meal which Helios and Mithra took on earth—though this may have been an imitation, rather than a forerunner, of the Christian Eucharist. (Liturgical documents are notoriously difficult to date.) When Paul of Tarsus spoke of being dead unto sin (Rom. 6:11), of newness of life (Rom. 6:4), when he declared that "the mind of the flesh is death; but the mind of the spirit is life and peace" (Rom. 8:6), he was using language which the devotees of the mystery religions would recognize and

[5] *The Pagan Background of Early Christianity*, p. 223.
[6] *Ibid.*, p. 303.

understand. When he declared that if he knew all mysteries, but had not love, he was nothing (I Cor. 13:2), he was speaking of something which was quite outside their range of experience.

Indeed the fundamental Christian experience was wholly different. It was Jewish rather than Hellenistic, and it was essentially historical. The idea of God as Saviour was in the Psalms as well as in the mystery religions. When the Roman emperor was worshiped, he was also called Saviour—and it can hardly be claimed that the Christians were imitators of the imperial cult!

The historical basis of primitive Christianity and the persistently Jewish character of New Testament thought, not least in St. Paul, have offered a stubborn resistance to the attempts to explain either as owing anything fundamental to contemporary heathenism. The most that we can say is that the literature of the mystery religions shews certain religious phraseology to have been current, and certain terms "in the air," at the time when the Christian Church took its rise.[7]

It is wholly understandable that Christian missionaries used this language; it is good evangelistic tactics to start with people where they are. Paul was ready to become all things to all men, if by any means he might win some (I Cor. 9:22). Needless to say he was not always successful. At Athens he tried to meet the philosophically-trained, novelty-seeking Athenians on their own

[7] E. G. Selwyn, *Epistle of Christian Courage; Studies in the First Epistle of St. Peter,* p. 305.

ground, with quotations from the philosophers to buttress his argument—but they did not really gather what he was driving at. Failure at Athens lay behind his decision that at Corinth he would stick to the plainest presentation of the gospel and know nothing but Jesus Christ and him crucified.

Did Christianity conquer because it was a mystery religion or because it was not? T. R. Glover's question answers itself. The resemblances between Christianity and the mysteries, though many and widespread, are superficial and easily explained. The differences lie deeper. First, the *mysteries were unhistorical;* they spoke of dying and rising gods, but no one really knew when these beings had lived and died and risen again. They were, indeed, but dramatizations of the recurring rhythm of the seasons, having their origin in vegetation myths. Winter was the death of the god, and spring his new life. But the Christian preachers were possessed by a quite different conviction: "That which was from the beginning, that which we have heard, that which we have seen with our eyes, . . . and our hands handled, concerning the Word of life . . . ; that which we have seen and heard declare we unto you" (I John 1:1, 3). Even Tacitus knew that the origins of Christianity were to be traced to one who was crucified under Pontius Pilate.

Secondly, *they were, on the whole, fashionable cults,* which, though promising moral power, had nothing of that grounding in the Ten Commandments which was the mark of Judaism and of Christianity. Christianity made a tremendous moral demand. It promised power

*47*

with which to meet it, and it won converts because that power was so impressively displayed by such unexpected people.

Thirdly, the *mystery cults were not exclusive in their demands*. You could worship Isis and the official Roman gods, and the emperor as well, when the need arose. Christianity was marked by what has been called "the scandal of particularity." It demanded the whole of a man's allegiance.

Stoicism was the chief form of philosophy current in the Hellenistic world. This also was part of the movement of thought from East to West, for nearly all the first Stoics were of Asiatic birth. The school was originated by Zeno, who came from Citium in Hellenized Cyprus to Athens about 350 years before Paul. Here he taught in the public colonnades (*stoai*) because he could not afford a private garden of his own. Stoicism was hardly, however, a clearly defined philosophical system; it was rather the inheritor, interpreter, and popularizer of earlier Greek thought. To this were added ideas of its own, and ideas which came from the East. Thus it accepted the cyclical view of history and the fatalism that went with it. It accepted the dualistic belief that the body was a tomb for the soul (*soma-sema* was the Greek catchword).

> Here in the body pent,
> Absent from Him I roam,

is sung by many a congregation at a watch-night service, but the idea it expresses is not a Christian one.

The later Stoicism also accepted the astrology of Iran. The universe, it was believed, consisted of heaven above heaven. If the soul was to make its progress to the seventh heaven, it must know the right names of the doorkeepers at each successive stage: and there were many worried people uncertain whether they could remember the difficult names aright. Some of these were later to welcome with relief the confident assertion that there was no name given under heaven by which men must be saved except the one name Jesus Christ (Acts 4:12). Christian martyrs died with the name of Jesus on their lips. They knew the only name that mattered.

The Stoics believed in God. Paul quoted one of their own writers, Aratus, from his own city of Tarsus, itself a notable center of Stoic teaching, who had said: "We are also his offspring" (Acts 17:28). But their belief in God faded into pantheism; it is an easy step from saying that God is in everything to saying that everything is God. Their God was not one who interfered in men's lives or acted upon the plane of history. Man must climb up the path of wisdom; he must try to be as like such a one as Socrates as he possibly could. But the way to do this was by living according to nature, by discovering the resources of strength and wisdom within himself.

> To thine own self be true,
> . . . . . . . . . . . . . . . . .
> Thou canst not then be false to any man.

This is Stoic doctrine—and it has nothing to say to man's blackest moods, when he begins to discover the depths of untruth within himself. Stoicism had no answer to the bitter experience of knowing the good and finding oneself inescapably impelled along the path of evil. "Who shall deliver me out of the body of this death?" (Rom. 7:24.) In the end the Stoic replied that you have to deliver yourself.

This strong sense of duty played a great part in the stabilization of the ancient world. Stoicism gave men a rough-and-ready way of facing life, and a high moral code. Its greatest good was not to be found in happiness but in doing what was right. The Stoic struggled to prevent himself from being swayed by his emotions. At the funeral of a loved one a simulated tear alone was permissible; it must not come from the heart. The agony in Gethsemane would mean to the Stoic nothing but failure; his system had no room for a Son of God "touched with the feeling of our infirmities" (Heb. 4: 15) . The attraction which Christianity possessed for sinners and outcasts seemed to the Stoics frankly immoral. For despite their universalism they never really liked the commonness of common people.

Nevertheless Stoicism helped to prepare the way for Christianity. The Stoics believed in one world which had no distinction between Greek and barbarian nor between slave and free. (The most influential Stoic teachers in the Roman period were the Emperor Marcus Aurelius and the slave Epictetus.) Paul appealed to their own beliefs when he said: "The God that made the world . . . made of one every nation of men for to dwell on all the face of the earth, . . . that they should seek after God, if haply they might feel after him, and find him, though he is not far from each of us: for in him we live, and move, and have our being" (Acts 17:24, 26-28). Christian ideals of behavior were to be indebted to the Stoic moralists. But not only did Christians set forward an ideal; they indicated the source of power through which that ideal might be attained. And because that power was clearly operative in their lives, both as individuals and as communities, they astonished the ancient world.

Throughout the Roman Empire the Jews were widely dispersed. It has been calculated that "in both Egypt and Syria there may well have been a million Jews, in Palestine 500,000, in the rest of the Roman Empire at least 1,500,000. If there were 55,000,000 inhabitants in the empire, at least 7 per cent of these must have been Jews." [8] The Greek geographer Strabo, who was on his travels when Jesus was born, said: "Jews were to be found in every city, and that in the whole world it was not easy to find a place where they had not penetrated and which was not dominated by them." [9] They were happy to live in Tarsus or Alexandria or Rome; they had no wish to settle on the highlands of Judea. Yet within them a highlander's loyalty burned as an unquenchable flame: "If I forget thee, O Jerusalem, let my right hand forget her cunning" (Ps. 137:5). To the outsider their attitude was one of conscious superiority. Three of the benedictions heard in their synagogues ran consecu-

[8] Hans Lietzmann, *The Beginning of the Christian Church*, p. 97.
[9] Josephus *Antiquities* 14.115.

tively: "Blessed be Thou who hast not made me a heathen; blessed be Thou who hast not made me a bondman; blessed be Thou who hast not made me a woman." In one of the earliest books of the New Testament one who had been a most zealous synagogue worshiper was to write: "There can be neither Jew nor Greek, there can be neither bond nor free, there can be no male and female: for ye are all one man in Christ Jesus" (Gal. 3:28).[10]

The Jews had a history of which they were proud, which they frequently recalled, and which spoke to them of God. They could never forget that he had delivered them out of Egypt and made of them a great and widespread people. But they had also the events of more recent history vivid in their memories. They were the one people whom neither Greece nor Rome had been able wholly to subdue or to assimilate. After the breakup of the empire of Alexander the descendants of one of his generals, Seleucus, were rulers in Syria. One of these was Antiochus Epiphanes—the name means *brilliant,* but behind his back there were some who called him Epimanes, or madman. He introduced Greek customs into Jerusalem; but though there were plenty of Jewish lads who were all for following the latest fashion, the conservative people of the country districts resisted to the death, and under the family of the Maccabees achieved freedom from foreign domination until their country passed under Rome in 63 B.C. An account of the

[10] See Israel Abrahams, "Rabbinic Aids to Exegesis," *Cambridge Biblical Essays,* p. 135.

struggle is to be found in the first book of Maccabees, in the Apocrypha. It was, no doubt, the exploits of these times which the author of Hebrews had in mind when he recalled that

others had trial of mockings and scourgings, yea, moreover of bonds and imprisonment: they were stoned, they were sawn asunder, they were tempted, they were slain with the sword: they went about in sheepskins, in goatskins; being destitute, afflicted, evil entreated (of whom the world was not worthy), wandering in deserts and mountains and caves, and the holes of the earth. (Heb. 11:36-38.)

A resistance movement inevitably produces its own kind of literature. That which was characteristic of the Jewish resistance to foreign oppression, whether Greek or Roman, is called *apocalyptic*. To the uninstructed it would have little meaning, but it was full of meaning for those who knew how to read its signs aright. It assured the Jewish reader of the ultimate triumph of God despite the temporary triumph of evil. The same kind of book found its place in the Christian New Testament under the title of the Revelation (or Apocalypse) of St. John the Divine. There is much similar material in the Gospels themselves; Mark 13 has been thought by many to be an apocalypse complete in itself. "But when ye see the abomination of desolation standing where he ought not (let him that readeth understand)" (vs. 14) is a typical direction to a reader of such books.

Yet among the Jews of the Dispersion were some who had a kindlier attitude toward Gentile culture. Contemporary with our Lord was a learned Jew named Philo, living in Alexandria, the great center of the new studies, who wrote at great length to prove that the Greek philosophers got what was true in their systems from the Jewish Law, that Moses was the greatest philosopher of them all. The older Hebrew tradition of wisdom was reinterpreted by others, and such books as the Wisdom of Solomon showed that all true wisdom came from God, that "the fear of the Lord is the beginning of wisdom." Even in Jerusalem the staid headmaster whose addresses are gathered together in the book of Ecclesiasticus essayed the same role. In Ecclesiastes—to which the Wisdom of Solomon may perhaps be a reply—skepticism even is linked with the Hebrew belief in the sovereignty of God.

Judaism at this time was a fervently missionary religion. The scribes and pharisees, said Jesus, would "compass sea and land to make one proselyte" (Matt. 23:15). There were those among its leaders who felt that it was called to become the one universal religion, who were looking for a Messiah who would be a light to lighten the Gentiles as well as the glory of his own people. "I will scatter this people among the Gentiles," said the Apocalypse of Baruch, "that they may do good to the Gentiles." There is evidence that this zeal was not without considerable effect. The Romans found it disturbing and annoying. None the less the Jews won special privileges from them. They were excused from appearance in a law court on a Saturday, and cases are known of Jewish soldiers being dispensed from military service on that day. The Jews found other ways of expressing loyalty to take the place of the imperial cult, and at one time a daily sacrifice for the emperor was offered in the temple at Jerusalem, according to Josephus.

To this privileged position of Judaism, Christianity was in some ways an heir. So long as it

was regarded as merely a variety of Judaism, it was actually protected by the Roman power, and owes no little of its original progress to the fact. In the Acts of the Apostles it is always from the Roman governor that St. Paul receives not only the fairest, but the most courteous treatment. It is the Jews who persecute him and work up difficulties against him, because to them he is a renegade and is weaning away their people.[11]

It was of Nero the Emperor that Paul wrote: "The powers that be are ordained of God" (Rom. 13:1). The time came speedily enough when the powers that be came to realize the threat to established ways which was implicit in the spread of the new faith. "It was just in this fact, that the Church claimed a different sanction, a separate life, and a new non-Roman unity, that lay the ground of the long persecution." [12] (Substitute *non-German, non-Japanese,* or *non-Russian* for non-Roman and you have a key to many problems in this new heroic age of Church history.) When this took place, the attitude of Christian writers changed, and the formerly beneficent

[11] T. G. Tucker, *Life in the Roman World of Nero and St. Paul,* p. 383.

[12] J. N. Figgis, *Churches in the Modern State,* p. 74.

power of Rome became the Great Beast of the book of Revelation.

The Jews won their proselytes. But it is more important for an understanding of the New Testament to realize that they won a far larger listening public. There are hints of this in the Gospels, especially in the centurion who sent Jewish elders to Jesus on behalf of his dying servant, that he might be healed. "And they, when they came to Jesus, besought him earnestly, saying, He is worthy that thou shouldest do this for him: for he loveth our nation, and himself built us our synagogue." (Luke 7:4-5.) In the Acts there are a number of places where those that feared God are mentioned. These were Gentiles, attracted by the noble monotheism of the Jews, but who had not yet taken the revolutionary step of becoming proselytes. Yet they attended the synagogue services Sabbath by Sabbath. In almost all the places where the Jews were dispersed these God-fearers were to be found. Wherever the missionaries went, they could find an audience, Gentile as well as Jewish, which was familiar with the Jewish Scriptures. When they declared to them that the Messiah had come, as foretold in the Scriptures, there was a considerable number of people who knew what the preachers were talking about. And though the Jews in the main resisted the new message, many God-fearers recognized that this was what they had been waiting for; what, through the mercy of God, they had been prepared for. We shall encounter these people again when we see a missionary party at work.

There was one of these God-fearers to whom the whole

Church owes very much. We can be pretty sure from Col. 4:14 that Luke was a Gentile. His name there occurs as one who was with Paul in his imprisonment; but a few verses earlier he had emphasized that a few others were the only ones "of the circumcision"—the only Jews, that is—who had remained as his fellow workers. Certainly Luke wrote some of the best Greek in the New Testament. But throughout it is the Greek of one who knew well the Old Testament in its Greek dress. The fact that so many Gentiles had thus been prepared for the Christian message was one of the special factors which enabled it to spread so rapidly.

# V

## The Missionary Message

THE Christian missionaries preached in a world which had been prepared for their message. Of this they were quite certain. "When the fulness of time came, God sent forth his Son." (Gal. 4:4.) They were themselves men "upon whom the ends of the ages are come" (I Cor. 10:11). God, who had spoken to earlier generations in limited, partial ways, had now "at the end of these days" spoken definitively in one who was a Son (Heb.1:1-2). Christian converts had already "tasted . . . the powers of the age to come" (Heb. 6:5). In the good news which they proclaimed, so these missionaries believed, the long history of the Hebrew people found its fulfillment, the frustrations of the Hellenistic age were resolved, the quick intellect of Greece taught true wisdom, the power of Rome brought before a mightier Power, whose ends it was called to serve. The new age was no longer something to dream about. It had come. They had witnessed its coming and must now tell other people all about it. To many beside the stupefied pagans of Lystra they could declare: "We . . . bring you good tidings, that ye should turn from these vain things unto the living God" (Acts 14:15).

That was how the Christian missionaries understood what they were about. Christian opinion today echoes their judgment. For us also the cleavage of history by the coming of Christ is that from which preceding and succeeding ages take their meaning. But what about those who first heard the astonishing story? Is it not natural that the majority regarded it as fantastic, that there were not in the first Christian communities "many of the wise (according to this world's judgment) nor many of the ruling class, nor many from the noblest families" (I Cor. 1:26)?[1] If the world had been prepared for the Christian message, it was usually only in the light of the acceptance of that message that the preparation could be discerned. The Christian faith did not arise naturally from Jewish expectation. It contradicted that expectation as all but very few Jews understood it. It did not arise naturally from pagan frustration. A god invented to meet the needs of the times would not really have suffered; he would have accepted one or other of the methods proposed by the tempter in the wilderness. If he had reached a cross, he would have left it triumphantly. "Was ever anything so absurd as a crucified deity? If Christendom had had its origin in a myth, it is inconceivable, wholly and absolutely inconceivable, that such a myth would resemble the Gospels, or that any legendary founder would have been in the least like Jesus."[2]

[1] J. B. Phillips, *Letters to Young Churches*. Copyright 1947 by the Macmillan Co., and used by their permission.

[2] C. E. Raven, *Jesus and the Gospel of Love*, p. 235.

This also the ablest of the preachers realized. Their crucified Messiah was, they believed, both the power of God and the wisdom of God. But the whole conception was a stumbling block to the Jews; it was here that nearly all of them tripped up. To the Gentiles it was foolishness. Nevertheless "it was God's good pleasure through the foolishness of the preaching [that is, of what was preached] to save them that believe" ( I Cor. 1:21) .

The word here translated preaching is the Greek *kerygma,* derived from *keryx,* meaning a herald or any public announcer. "A *keryx* may be a town crier, an auctioneer, a herald, or anyone who lifts up his voice and claims public attention to some definite thing he has to announce" [3]—which is exactly what Paul of Tarsus did in the synagogues, where his announcement usually ended in expulsion, in Athens, where it only produced derision, in courtroom, sailing ship, or prison, in season, out of season. His announcement was definite, concrete, startling. He told men what God had done.

And what had God done? When Paul wrote to the church in Corinth, he recalled the message which had been the basis of his campaign. "I make known unto you, brethren, the gospel which I preached unto you, which also ye received, wherein also ye stand." (I Cor. 15:1-2.) This measured introduction leads to a statement which reads almost like a creed. "For I delivered unto you first of all that which also I received, how that Christ died

---

[3] C. H. Dodd, *The Apostolic Preaching and Its Developments,* p. 4.

for our sins according to the scriptures; and that he was buried; and that he hath been raised on the third day according to the scriptures; and that he appeared to Cephas." (I Cor. 15:3-5.) The successive "and that . . . and that . . . and that . . . and that" is not due to poor translation; it represents a Greek word which sometimes served the purpose for which in English we employ the useful device of quotation marks. That is to say, it looks as if Paul might here be quoting. If so, what?

It is possible that he is reminding the Corinthian Christians of a summary of his own teaching which he has left behind for them to learn by heart. But the statement is described as "that which also I received." This has led to the conjecture that what is here embedded in the letter to Corinth is the summary of the Christian faith which Paul was taught when he was himself a new convert, when "he was certain days with the disciples which were at Damascus" (Acts 9:19). This would mean that we have here a portion, at any rate, of the primitive Christian faith as the church in Damascus accepted it— and the fact that Peter's name is here given in its Aramaic rather than its Greek form, which would be much more familiar in Corinth, lends support to this suggestion. Afterward the quotation marks cease as Paul adds further cumulative evidence of the resurrection of Christ: "Then to the twelve; then he appeared to above five hundred brethren at once, of whom the greater part remain until now, but some are fallen asleep; then he appeared to James; then to all the apostles; and last of all, as unto one born out of due time, he appeared to me also" (I Cor. 15:6-8) .[4]

This was the basis of Paul's preaching, a generally accepted Christian belief given an electric significance through his own personal experience. He made no claim to natural eloquence; he spoke not because he had great oratorical gifts but because it was impossible to keep silence (see I Cor. 2:1-8; 9:16) . Nor was his preaching effective merely because of the story he told. It was effective only because the living Christ was with him as he spoke. The story was a recital of events in history. But they were more than historical events; they were related to history's beginning and its end. All happened, as we read in one of Peter's speeches, "by the deliberate counsel and foreknowledge of God" (Acts 2:23) . It was all "according to the scriptures."

This was not all that Paul received from those who had been Christians before him. Sometimes, as we shall see, he was able to meet his converts' questions about conduct with a "word of the Lord." It is to Paul that we owe the earliest, and in some ways the fullest, account of the institution of the Eucharist (I Cor. 11:23-25) . This account is prefaced by the words: "I received of the Lord that which also I delivered unto you." This might mean that the apostle was claiming that the risen Christ was the direct and immediate source of his information. But this is hardly likely. As H. L. Goudge put it, he "received the historical facts of the Gospel from the

[4] Throughout the previous two paragraphs I am indebted to Professor William Robinson of the Selly Oak Colleges.

Apostles, and the spiritual meaning of those facts from the Lord Himself." [5] The statement goes on, "How that the Lord Jesus in the night in which he was betrayed took bread"— which not only refers to the Lord Jesus in the third person but looks like the opening of a traditional and often repeated statement. It was in worship that the words of Jesus would be frequently and formally recalled. These words form the basis of the consecration prayer in the service of Holy Communion. They may well have had the same place in the worship of the church at Corinth, when Paul was there, in the years A.D. 51-53.

Paul's letters to Corinth and to other churches thus reveal clear evidence of some of the bare bones of the Christian message by which and to which members of the earliest churches outside Palestine itself were converted. But what of the Christians in our Lord's own land? What were the beliefs of the church in Jerusalem? Have we any evidence of these? We believe that we have.

This evidence is to be found in a number of speeches recorded in the book of Acts and attributed in the main to Peter. (See Acts 2:14-39; 3:13-26; 4:10-12; 5:30-32; 10:36-43; 13:17-41. The last of these speeches is attributed to Paul. With these should be compared the speech of Stephen in Acts 7:2-53.) In the opening of his Gospel—the first volume, of which the book of Acts is the second—Luke laid claim to being a careful historian, to have considered many written documents, and to have

[5] *Westminster Commentary* on I Cor. 15:3.

"traced the course of all things accurately from the first."
Some recent scholars believe that in these speeches he
made use of early documents originally written, not in
Greek, but in Aramaic. This is particularly noticeable
in the speech to Cornelius in Acts 10:36-43. Luke wrote
some of the best Greek in the New Testament; but the
Greek of this passage, says Professor A. M. Hunter, "almost defies translation," but when put back into Aramaic "becomes tolerably perspicuous." [6] Let us look at
this passage:

The word which he sent unto the children of Israel,
preaching good tidings of peace by Jesus Christ (he is Lord
of all) —that saying ye yourselves know, which was published throughout all Judea, beginning from Galilee, after
the baptism which John preached; even Jesus of Nazareth,
how that God anointed him with the Holy Ghost and with
power: who went about doing good, and healing all that
were oppressed of the devil; for God was with him. And
we are witnesses of all things which he did both in the
country of the Jews, and in Jerusalem; whom also they
slew, hanging him on a tree. Him God raised up the third
day, and gave him to be made manifest, not to all the
people, but unto witnesses that were chosen before of God,
even to us, who did eat and drink with him after he rose
from the dead. And he charged us to preach unto the people,
and to testify that this is he which is ordained of God to
be the Judge of quick and dead. To him bear all the
prophets witness, that through his name every one that be-
lieveth on him shall receive remission of sins.

Here, once again, is a recital of facts in history which
have a meaning which lies beyond history. This was the

[6] *The Unity of the New Testament*, p. 23.

gospel as the early Church in Jerusalem understood it.

When we examine this speech and its parallels in detail, we can analyze the missionary message under a series of headings.

1. *The age which the prophets foretold has come.* This was a claim which all those who had been nurtured on the Hebrew Scriptures would understand. The existence of the many circles of God-fearers meant that there were thousands of men and women from the Gentile world who had already taken first steps in the direction of Christianity. All who heard the message were made to realize that they were living in a critical season which called for decisive action.

2. *This happened through Jesus Christ.* Jesus was his human name; we are accustomed to the Hebrew form of it as Joshua. The word "Christ" was not a name but a title, though it soon came to be treated as a second name. It means "the anointed one" and is the Greek translation of the Hebrew "Messiah." It was thus the very foundation of the missionary preaching that Jesus was the Messiah. But the account which followed showed how he contradicted Jewish expectation. Although he demonstrated that he was "approved of God unto you by mighty works and wonders and signs, which God did by him" (Acts 2:22), although he "went about doing good, and healing all that were oppressed of the devil; for God was with him" (Acts 10:38), nevertheless in the end the religious leaders of his country slew him, "hanging him on a tree" (Acts 5:30), the symbol of one not approved but rejected by God. Man's victory provided God's op-

portunity. It was not possible that God's chosen should be holden by death; God raised him up on the third day.

3. *Jesus has been exalted to the right hand of God.* The stone which was set at nought by the builders—the hearers would pick up at once the reference to Ps. 118—has become the headstone of the corner (Acts 4:11). He is prince of life and Saviour of men (Acts 5:31).[7]

4. *The exaltation of Jesus has been followed by an outpouring of the Holy Spirit.* The idea of the Holy Spirit was not new. Luke records that Jesus preached his first sermon in the synagogue at Nazareth from the text in Isaiah: "The Spirit of the Lord is upon me" (Luke 4:18). The word "Spirit" means literally breath or wind; it thus conveys the sense both of life and of invisible power constantly at work. The Christian missionaries believed that the Spirit had inspired the prophets, but they were also convinced that they had themselves experienced a new and abiding manifestation of the Spirit, who was the very Spirit of Jesus. He had promised that a Paraclete—one called to a man's side to help him—would take his place after his physical presence was withdrawn from his followers (see John 14–16), and that promise had been fulfilled. The work of the Holy Spirit in the Church was the evidence of Christ's power and glory. The Jewish members of the Church had to learn, to their amazement, that the same experience was offered to Gentiles as to them (Acts 10:45).

5. *The exalted Christ will shortly return to the world*

[7] Cf. Acts 3:15. The word translated "prince" often means originator or founder. Cf. Heb. 12:2.

*once again to consummate his work.* If we are to understand the New Testament, we must bear in mind this unfulfilled expectation of the early Church. It is, for example, the reason the written Gospels were not written earlier. Men do not write for posterity when they believe that there will be no posterity to write for. Yet it is clear that during the lifetime of Paul his attitude in this matter changed. When he wrote I Thessalonians, he was expecting a speedy return of Christ. When he wrote Ephesians, he was working out a philosophy of history, looking forward through ages to come.

6. *The message ended with a challenge to repentance.* The word for repentance in the New Testament means "thinking things out afresh," "starting out in a new direction." What the preachers sought was no mere intellectual exercise; it was a life decision, to be taken when history itself was at its most decisive hour. Behind the Greek word there lies the Hebrew idea of "turning to God" [8]; men were called to turn to God and think things out afresh in the light of his new revelation of himself in Jesus. Those who would do so were offered the immediate experience of the Holy Spirit and the assurance that their sins were forgiven. Through baptism they entered the new fellowship of the Church. Paul emphasizes again and again in his letters the decisiveness of the act which the Christians had made; his use of the aorist tense makes clear the "once for all" nature of what had taken place. Christ had died; in baptism they too had died to the world. He had risen from the dead; in baptism they also

[8] Cf. R. Newton Flew, *Jesus and His Church,* p. 50, n. 2.

had entered upon a new life; they lived and died as men *in* Christ. The often-repeated missionary message becomes the basis for a life in which the baser passions of life are mortified:

If then ye were raised together with Christ, seek the things that are above, where Christ is, seated on the right hand of God. Set your mind on the things that are above, not on the things that are upon the earth. For ye died, and your life is hid with Christ in God. When Christ, who is our life, shall be manifested, then shall ye also with him be manifested in glory. (Col. 3:1-4.)

There is a popular hymn which begins, "We've a story to tell to the nations." That is exactly what the missionary preaching was. We have analyzed some of the bare bones of this story—realizing, it is to be hoped, that those who first told it clothed it with far more flesh and blood than we have been able to recover. Nor should we be right to think that the story was almost exclusively one of a death and burial and resurrection. We shall find that Paul even was much more familiar with the teaching of Jesus than is sometimes supposed. It is to be remembered that one who accompanied him on many of his travels was Luke, already gathering the materials which were to be given such exquisite literary form in his Gospel. When Matthias was chosen by lot to fill the place vacated by Judas Iscariot in the ranks of the twelve, he was not chosen only as a witness of the Resurrection. It was also emphasized that he should be one who knew the whole of the ministry of Jesus.

Of the men therefore which have companied with us all the time that the Lord Jesus went in and went out among us, beginning from the baptism of John, unto the day that he was received up from us, of these must one become a witness with us of his resurrection. (Acts 1:21-22.)

It is the Christian claim that what man could not do, God has done; that God has once for all acted in a special series of events in history in such a way as to show men forever what he is like, and to create for all men the possibility of immediate and developing fellowship with him. As Archbishop William Temple once put it, "The difference between Catholic and Protestant is very small as compared with the difference between Christian and non-Christian, between those who do and those who do not believe that in Jesus Christ God hath visited and redeemed His people." [9] It is here, in this realm of belief, that the essential difference lies, and not in the realm of conduct, although the belief expresses itself in conduct. The tree is known by its fruits, but there are no fruits without the tree.

What we have discovered in a few references to Paul's letters and in the speeches in the book of Acts is the basis of the *whole* New Testament. This is the story which was told to the nations. This is what the Jews tripped up over, what decently educated people mostly regarded as foolishness. "Like a song which keeps sounding in our heads in all sorts of circumstances, we hear again and again the authentic notes of the *kerygma* ring

[9] *The Church Looks Forward*, p. 32.

out in gospel, epistle, and homily." [10] Although the written Gospels fill out so greatly our knowledge of the early ministry and teaching of Jesus, the shadow of the Cross falls early on the story; only the accounts of the Passion and Resurrection are at all fully detailed—for those who wrote them did so from the same point of view as the missionary preachers announced their stupendous news. We shall find that the most concise summary of it all is early in the Gospel of Mark: "Now after that John was delivered up, Jesus came into Galilee, preaching the gospel of God, and saying, The time is fulfilled, and the kingdom of God is at hand: repent ye, and believe in the gospel" (1:14). Professor Hunter has also written: "In a true sense the rest of the New Testament is commentary on this verse." [11] The Fourth Gospel sets forth the purpose of it all: "These things are written, that ye may believe that Jesus is the Christ, the Son of God; and that believing ye may have life in his name" (20:31). *The key to the understanding of the New Testament documents is that they are the propagandist literature of a widespread and successful missionary movement.* Behind the written propaganda lay the spoken propaganda, and through it the Church was built up. It was the preaching of the gospel which won men to the Church; later the Church itself was to produce the written Gospels which it needed.

[10] Hunter, *op. cit.,* p. 25.
[11] *Torch Commentary* on Mark, p. 31.

# VI

## Establishing the Converts

ONE of the questions which need to be answered if any missionary movement is to be understood is: *If the mission is at all successful, we must try to discover what are the factors, in the message itself, in the life which it produces, and in the circumstances of the time, which contribute to that success.* Sufficient evidence was brought together in earlier chapters for us to realize how the message which we have considered in the last one met the basic needs of the time—and, it might be added, of our own time and of every time. What of the life which the message produced? That also is a matter of importance, for the first century and for every century.

The earliest converts were won to the Christian faith by the proclamation of the missionary message. Here were speakers who, like the Master they served, spoke with a note of authority. "The Rabbis taught, and nothing happened. Jesus taught, and all kinds of things happened." [1] This was true of his followers also. The poor had the gospel preached to them—and when this

[1] Manson, *op. cit.*, p. 35.

was done, the blind received their sight, the lame walked, the lepers were cleansed, and the deaf heard (cf. Matt. 11:5; Luke 7:22). Paul could remind the Corinthian Christians that though he might not have announced his message very eloquently, yet he had done so "in demonstration of the Spirit and of power" (I Cor. 2:4). The Thessalonians were similarly reminded of how Paul and Silvanus and Timothy had preached to them when they came smarting with the wounds of Philippi: "Our gospel came not unto you in word only, but also in power, and in the Holy Spirit, and in much assurance" (I Thess. 1:5). More lasting than the works of healing was the effect of the preaching in producing a changed moral life. In this there were no wonder-workers who could claim to rival them.

There lay the great surprise. The Christians came with a message of the highest conceivable morality to men and women who had failed to satisfy even the abridged standards of a pagan city, to men and women of broken will, "hardened to stone" and "past feeling," as even the Stoics said. They expected a response; they preached repentance and reformation; and people did respond, they repented and they lived new lives.[2]

In the second century, when Christian writers defended their faith against the attacks of pagans, it was to this fact of moral reformation that they could confidently turn for their most clinching argument:

Christians do not differ from mankind at large either in territory, in language, or in their way of life. They observe

___

[2] T. R. Glover, *The Influence of Christ in the Ancient World*, p. 75.

local customs, and practise no strange fashions; yet for all that there is something about them which is peculiar to themselves. Thus: they dwell each in his own country, but only as pilgrims and sojourners. They share the same duties as their fellow-citizens, yet suffer every indignity as foreigners. Every foreign land is, for them, a fatherland, and every fatherland is foreign. They are in the flesh, but live not after the flesh. They obey the laws while passing their days on earth, but their citizenship is in heaven. They love all men—and are persecuted by all. Doing good, they are penalized as doers of evil, assaulted by Jews as foreigners, by heathen as fit subjects for attack. And those that hate them can assign no reason for their hatred. In a word— what the soul is to the body, the Christians are to the world. And mark this: the greater the number of those persecuted, the more does the number of the rest increase. Surely these things are not the works of men; they are the power of God, and the tokens of His divine presence.[8]

The moral power displayed by the Christian converts was new. The life they lived in common was new also. There is no more notable New Testament word than *koinonia*—so inadequately translated *fellowship*. The Hellenistic world ached for friendship; its pain was partly assuaged by the various associations which met under the title of *"collegia tenuiorum,"* or poor men's burial clubs. "These colleges," says Sir Samuel Dill, "became homes for the homeless, a little fatherland or *patria* for those without a country." [4] In them the social divisions of the outside world were forgotten. "Distinctions there

[8] *Epistle to Diognetus.* This cento from chs. 5-7 is in the introductory notes to E. H. Blakeney's edition of the Greek text.

[4] *Roman Society from Nero to Marcus Aurelius,* p. 271.

were, but they were the distinctions of seniority in the society, not those of wealth or rank outside. Slaves had an equal voice with free-born members at the meetings, and might rise to be officers of the society in due course." [5] Our own world has been particularly fruitful in producing similar societies—not usually styled burial clubs—to meet a similar need, and these have often been influenced by the Christian ethic of service to others. Those in the ancient world were, however, inward-looking; they spent their money on their own objects, not on relieving the poor and aged. That came in with Christianity, though a pagan emperor, Julian, imitated it. Nor were these clubs based upon a particular belief; theirs was the genial good fellowship of those who say, "The more we are together the merrier we'll be." They represented, none the less, the hunger that men felt for a society in which all distinctions would be permanently transcended.

What mattered in the Christian society was not circumcision, nor uncircumcision, but men reborn in Christ (Gal. 6:15). In it the Holy Spirit was growing his own characteristic harvest—love, joy, peace, longsuffering, kindness, goodness, faithfulness, meekness, temperance (Gal. 5:22). Those who had decisively bidden farewell to the old life and entered, at baptism, upon a new one were united by a bond which no outside force could break. "For as many of you as were baptized into Christ did put on Christ. There can be neither Jew nor Greek, there can be neither bond nor free,

[5] Halliday, *op. cit.,* p. 61.

there can be no male and female: for ye are all one man in Christ Jesus." (Gal. 3:28.) This was Paul's special message, frequently reiterated. "For Christ is our living Peace. He has made a unity of the conflicting elements of Jew and Gentile by breaking down the barrier which lay between us." (Eph. 2:14.) [6] But the same point was made by Peter. He wrote to those "which in time past were no people"—a heterogeneous group with very varied backgrounds—"but are now the people of God: which had not obtained mercy, but now have obtained mercy" (I Pet. 2:10) . The new people—the third race, as some were to call it—was not self-created, a group of men and women associating because they found each other congenial; in it quite uncongenial types were brought together by the same inward compulsion. It was the result of God's initiative, brought to birth through the harsh travail of Calvary.

In the new power which the Christians displayed, in the new life of fellowship which they revealed, lay causes for the success of the Christian mission as it pressed beyond the circles of Jews and God-fearers. Men heard the message—and at first it seemed a strange one, expressed in alien categories. They saw the Church—and they felt compelled to pay fresh attention to the message which lay behind it. As the late Edwyn Bevan put it in a passage which has been often quoted:

It can hardly be doubted that the attraction of Christianity from the very beginning was social. It was not as dis-

[6] J. B. Phillips, *Letters to Young Churches*. Copyright 1947 by the Macmillan Co., and used by their permission.

embodied truth uttered into the air that the Christian "Good News" laid hold of men; it was through the corporate life of the little Christian societies in the cities of the ancient world. The life and spirit of these societies was indeed what it was because amongst them the Christian Good News was believed, but it was the life and spirit which gave the Good News its power. Men coming into contact with such a group felt an atmosphere unlike anything else. Each little group was a centre of attraction which drew men in from the surrounding world. In that way, probably, more than by the preaching of any few individuals, the Church grew.[7]

For this new society there were several names. It was known, in the first place, as the Way, a term which comprehended both the believers and their belief, and which at the same time emphasized that this belief must have results in action (see Acts 9:2; 18:25-26; 19:9, 23; 22:4; 24:14, 22). When Paul wrote to the churches in Rome, Corinth, Ephesus—if that was the destination of Ephesians, which is unlikely—Philippi, and Colossae, he wrote to men and women whom he addressed as "saints." The root idea of the word is consecration, of people set apart for God, to be exclusively his. It does not mean that they were specially good; they were people, on the contrary, who recognized that God had been especially good to them, but who remained in daily need of his grace. Another term which Paul used—with great courage—was in calling the Church the body of Christ. Those who were faithful to Christ were used by him as limbs. John Baillie says:

[7] *Christianity*, p. 51.

We speak very easily and familiarly nowadays of being a "member" of this or that society. But we ought never to forget that this usage had its origin, as it still has its only full and real meaning, in the Church of Christ. The Church was the first society of which men spoke of themselves as being members, and when it was first used by St. Paul this must have seemed a very startling, and even extravagant, manner of speech.[8]

The word most commonly used was *ekklesia*, which we rightly translate Church. In classical Greek the word could be used of any assembly; this led Tyndale to translate it *congregacyon*. A study of its use in the New Testament makes it clear that it means far more than this. The translators of the King James Version—and of the earlier Geneva Bible—reverted to the word Church, which had been used by Wycliffe. Behind the use of the Greek *ekklesia* lay the Hebrew *qahal*, which was "used to signify, not an assembly of Israel upon some particular occasion, but the people of Israel as God's People, distinct from everybody else, whether assembled or unassembled, the chosen of Jehovah for His service." [9] There were not many holy nations; there was only one. There was only one Church, exemplified in many local groupings.

When the word *ekklesia* is used in the New Testament, it is with conscious reference to this Old Testament conception. One can hardly say, therefore, that Jesus

[8] *Invitation to Pilgrimage,* p. 121.

[9] Sir Edwyn Hoskyns and Noel Davey, *The Riddle of the New Testament,* p. 30.

founded the Church. The truth rather is that He redeemed the Church. For centuries there had been a people who looked upon themselves as set apart for God. When Christians applied the term *ekklesia* to themselves they re-defined the People of God in terms of the new acts of God for their redemption. It was not to be identified with Israel after the flesh, but with individuals from every tribe, nation, people, and tongue. (Rev. 7:9, etc.) Its adherents were not those who were strictly loyal to Torah, for Christ was the end of the law (Rom. 10:4). Its center was not in a Temple where sacrifices were continually offered, but in Christ Who had died for their sins and been raised from the dead (I Cor. 15:3 ff.). Though membership in the People of God was determined by different criteria, the basic conception of a Church goes back to the Old Testament. The true Remnant about which the prophets had spoken, had found fulfillment in the Christian community.[10]

Faraway places and ages distant in time have a particular fascination for many people. We tend to see the early Church, or the Church in the mission field, through romantic, rose-colored spectacles, while donning smoked glasses for looking at the Church in its more immediate local manifestations. In some books of missionary propaganda it was customary to print photographs of converts which the reader was asked to contrast with other photographs of similar natives "in their pagan state." The difference was obvious, and very real; but the impression was sometimes half unconsciously conveyed that they retained forever the expressions with which they had confronted the photographer.

[10] Clarence T. Craig in *The Universal Church in God's Design* (Amsterdam Assembly Series), p. 33.

The same missionaries who testify to the remarkable effects of the gospel upon converts are the first to declare that after conversion all is not plain sailing. Old forces lurk unsuspected; old customs retain their hold; old lures attract. Paul of Tarsus could write to his Corinthian converts: "Ye are our epistle, written in our hearts, known and read of all men" (II Cor. 3:2). But he could also accuse them of party spirit (I Cor. 1:10-17), of saying hard things about him behind his back which they would never have dared say to his face (II Cor. 10:10-18), of drunkenness upon most solemn occasions (I Cor. 11:21), of harboring an unsavory case of incest (I Cor. 5:1-13). He explains that he had to give them baby food, and is disappointed that they are so far from being ready for solid meat. Almost all his epistles were called forth by failure of some kind—moral failure, or failure to grasp true teaching, or the failure which is implicit in a readiness to take up every new religious fad. The same causes remain operative in missionary work today.

We begin now to understand how shocking it was to many Jewish Christians when Paul of Tarsus declared that it was not necessary for Gentile converts to be subjected to the full rigors of the Jewish Law. That, they must have felt, was exactly what was needed. After all, Paul himself, their evangelist and champion, had few illusions about them. What sort of people were these converts of his? Not "many of the wise (according to this world's judgment) nor many of the ruling class, nor

many from the noblest families." (I Cor. 1:26.) [11]
It was wonderful that they had been brought to
Christ. But consider their past! Could anyone doubt that
what they needed was discipline? Why discard God's
appointed method, the Jewish Law? Paul said: "Believe
on the Lord Jesus and thou shalt be saved" (Acts 16:31).
To this proposition the "Judaizing" party added a tremendous rider: "Except ye be circumcised and walk
after the custom of Moses, ye cannot be saved" (Acts
15:1, Bezan text).

The sharpness of the ensuing controversy, which fills
the Epistle to the Galatians and overshadows much else
of Paul's writings, has obscured the fact that Paul did
indeed believe in discipline, that he handed on to his
Gentile converts the essential parts of the Jewish moral
tradition. To him circumcision—the rite of admission
into the Jewish community—was not really important,
though he caused the half-Jewish Timothy to be circumcised so that he might have freedom of entry into
the synagogues, and so that he might not appear to be
ostentatiously flouting national tradition. But when it
came to the Ten Commandments it was quite another
matter.

His epistles usually contain theological argumenta-
tion in their earlier sections and direct moral teaching
toward the end. They were designed to be read in
churches; it is a cause of astonishment to uninstructed
modern congregations that their first-century counter-

[11] J. B. Phillips, *Letters to Young Churches*. Copyright 1947 by the
Macmillan Co., and used by their permission.

parts should be able to follow such intricate technical reasoning at the first hearing. Not all, of course, could. To some of the not very wise it must have been extremely difficult. But they listened intently—perhaps they even woke up—when the later sections were read out. It might be a direct instruction to two women in Philippi to stop bickering. It might be the bald direction: "Let him that stole steal no more: but rather let him labor, working with his hands the thing that is good, that he may have whereof to give to him that hath need" (Eph. 4:28) .

A missionary separated from those whom he has brought to the faith finds himself obliged to say two things repeatedly. He must say, "Remember what I taught you." He must also say, what in another man might seem conceited, "Remember what I did." They have had only one outline of the Christian faith; they have seen only one expert in Christian living. It is important that they should not forget what was taught directly and what was taught by example. In Hebrew thought the conception of expressing one's belief in daily life was expressed by the verb "to walk." Christians similarly were besought "to walk worthily of the calling wherewith [they] were called, with all lowliness and meekness, . . . forbearing one another in love; giving diligence to keep the unity of the Spirit in the bond of peace" (Eph. 4:1-3) . To the church at Philippi, Paul wrote: "Brethren, be ye imitators together of me, and mark them which so walk even as ye have us for an ensample" (3:17) . To the Corinthians he wrote: "Be ye imitators of me, even as I also am of Christ" (I Cor. 11:1). To Christians at Thessalonica, restless and excited by anticipation of the coming End of the Age, he wrote paradoxically: "Study to be quiet, and to do your own business, and to work with your hands, even as we charged you; that ye may walk honestly toward them that are without, and may have need of nothing" (I Thess. 4:11-12). In his second letter to the same church he reminded them of how he and Silvanus and Timothy had worked with their hands day and night: "To make ourselves an ensample unto you, that ye should imitate us. For even when we were with you, this we commanded you, If any man will not work, neither let him eat" (II Thess. 3:9-10; see also Rom. 6:4; II Cor. 5:7; Gal. 6:16; Eph. 5:15; Col. 1:10; I Thess. 2:12; 4:1).

Paul's attitude to the Law, he might have claimed, was fundamentally the same as his Master's. He was engaged, not in destroying, but in fulfilling the Law and the Prophets. He was working out in practice what the fulfillment meant. He wrote to Rome:

Owe no man anything, save to love one another: for he that loveth his neighbour hath fulfilled the law. For this, Thou shalt not commit adultery, . . . Thou shalt not steal, Thou shalt not covet, and if there be any other commandment, it is summed up in this word, namely, Thou shalt love thy neighbour as thyself. (Rom. 13:8-9; cf. Gal. 5:14.)

There was simple moral teaching which had to be pressed home again and again, and most of it was in a form with which Paul was familiar since he was a boy at school in the synagogue at Tarsus.

Any evangelist of a community which newly accepts his message, for example some outcaste village community in India, quickly reaches a stage at which the most urgent need is to expound quite simply what the new-found creed implies for practical life. How must people behave who believe in one God of righteousness—that is the question he has to answer. Very often he finds himself making a large use for these very Ten Commandments. The fact that all over the world they are employed in instruction before or after baptism is significant, and a striking proof that they represent the rudiments of religious education.[12]

With these same simple lessons the Gentile converts in the early Church were taught to walk in the new Way. If we take the Ten Commandments as our guide, we shall find that each of them was emphasized by the apostle in teaching or in practice. In a short book this cannot be an exhaustive study. And if the examples used are chosen from the writings of Paul, we have to remember that similar teaching was being given by other missionaries in other centers, though not on the whole by men whose writings have been preserved for our inspection.

1. *I am the Lord thy God: Thou shalt have none other gods but me.* That is, of course, the assumed basis of Paul's teaching. It is expressed in his speech at Athens: "What therefore ye worship in ignorance, this I set forth unto you. The God that made the world and all things therein, he, being Lord of heaven and earth, dwelleth not in temples made with hands" (Acts 17:23-24) . The first

[12] Godfrey E. Phillips, *The Old Testament in the World Church*, p. 42.

chapter of Romans is full of his poignant sorrow over the pagan world around him, which had failed to live by the best light which it had been given, "because that, knowing God, they glorified him not as God, neither gave thanks; but became vain in their reasonings, and their senseless heart was darkened" (1:21). In the same epistle he quotes from Ps. 36, applying its condemnation to both Jews and Greeks: "There is no fear of God before their eyes" (3:18). And he argues: "Is God the God of Jews only? is he not the God of Gentiles also? . . . God is one" (3:29-30). But his monotheism is more fitly expressed in the language of worship than in that of argument: "O the depth of the riches, both of the wisdom and the knowledge of God! how unsearchable are his judgements, and his ways past tracing out!" (Rom. 11:33).

2. *Thou shalt not make to thyself any graven image.* The old Jewish fear of idolatry is expressed in the injunction made by the Council of Jerusalem concerning Gentile converts: "That they abstain from the pollution of idols" (Acts 15:20). In Galatians idolatry is listed as one of the works of the flesh (5:20). In Ephesians it is stated that no "covetous man, which is an idolater, hath any inheritance in the kingdom of Christ" (5:5). (This passage, which begins "For this ye know of a surety," looks as if it might be a reminder of a form of teaching learned by heart, based upon the Commandments.) In I Corinthians idolaters appear in another list of those who shall not inherit the kingdom of God (6:9). Later in the epistle comes the injunction, "Neither be ye

idolaters" (10:7), and the plea, "Wherefore, my beloved, flee from idolatry" (10:14).

3. *Thou shalt not take the Name of the Lord thy God in vain.* "Let no corrupt speech proceed out of your mouth," we read in Eph. 4:29, and in II Cor. 4:2: "We have renounced the hidden things of shame, not walking in craftiness, nor handling the word of God deceitfully; but by the manifestation of the truth commending ourselves to every man's conscience in the sight of God." In Rom. 1:31 "convenant-breakers" are listed among the evil manifestations of the Gentile world.

4. *Remember that thou keep holy the Sabbath.* This command is nowhere specifically enjoined; the only reference to the Sabbath is a critical one to Christians influenced by Judaism who are making too much of it (Col. 2:16). But Paul's practice is clear from Acts. The Sabbath found him in the synagogue, endeavoring to tell others about Jesus the Messiah (see Acts 13:14, 42; 15:21; 16:13; 17:2). In I Cor. 16:1—immediately after his great passage on the Resurrection—is the first reference to Sunday, the first day of the week, as one when Christians met. The phrase "the Lord's day" is to be found in Rev. 1:10. "Jewish Christians would at first observe both the Sabbath on Saturday, and 'the first day of the week' as the day of the Lord's Resurrection. Gentile Christians never, as far as we know, observed the Sabbath at all." [13]

[13] H. L. Goudge on I Cor. 16:2.

5. *Honour thy father and thy mother.* This is specifically enjoined in Eph. 6:2, where it is described as "the first commandment with promise." In Col. 3:20 we read, "Children, obey your parents in all things, for this is well-pleasing in the Lord." Among the evil manifestations of the Gentile world in Rom. 1:30 are those who are "disobedient to parents."

6. *Thou shalt do no murder.* Murders are listed among the works of the flesh in Gal. 5:21. Murder is a further evil manifestation of the Gentile world in Rom. 1:29. "Murderers" come in a rather similar list in I Timothy of those against whom the law is designed (1:8-11). None of this was directed to the new converts, who might be supposed to be above this particular temptation. It was left to a later teacher to spiritualize the commandment: "Whosoever hateth his brother is a murderer: and ye know that no murderer hath eternal life abiding in him" (I John 3:15).

7. *Thou shalt not commit adultery.* Impurity was particularly prevalent in the cities in which the gospel was proclaimed, and warnings against it abound in the epistles. The summary is to be found in Eph. 5:3: "But fornication, and all uncleanness, or covetousness, let it not even be named among you, as becometh saints." The positive side of this is to be found in the same chapter: "Husbands, love your wives, even as Christ also loved the church, and gave himself up for it" (5:25). The language is so familiar that we hardly notice its boldness or its superlatively high estimate of the marriage relationship. Marriage presented problems to the

early Christians. Some of these are dealt with in I Cor. 7 (see also Gal. 5:19; Col. 3:5; I Thess. 4:4-7; Rom. 2:22; 7:3; 13:9; I Cor. 5:1-13; 6:9, 13-20; 10:8; II Cor. 12:21).

8. *Thou shalt not steal.* We have already read in Eph. 4:28, "Let him that stole steal no more," with its practical suggestion of a better use for hands that might otherwise get into mischief.

9. *Thou shalt not bear false witness against thy neighbour.* In Ephesians is the phrase "speaking truth in love" (4:15) and the definite command, with an indication of its social consequences, of what it means to be a neighbor: "Wherefore, putting away falsehood, speak ye truth each one with his neighbour: for we are members one of another" (4:25). The catalogue of what the Philippian Christians are called to meditate upon begins with "whatsoever things are true" (4:8).

10. *Thou shalt not covet.* Covetousness is much reprobated by Paul, and often linked with idolatry. It is a mark of evil in the Gentile world (Rom. 1:29). It is the sin which springs most instantly to mind to illustrate the effect of the law. "I had not known sin, except through the law: for I had not known coveting, except the law had said, Thou shalt not covet." (Rom. 7:7.) One of the evil passions to be mortified by those who are raised together with Christ is "covetousness, which is idolatry" (Col. 3:5).

Paul did not teach only the negative commandments to his converts. The positive Beatitudes may also be found embedded in his teaching. But their discovery must be left as a profitable exercise for the reader's leisure. There is one beatitude which none of the Gospels record, but which Luke reports as quoted in a speech by Paul. When he bade farewell to the elders at Miletus, he recalled the three years he had taught them day and night at Ephesus, declaring to them the whole counsel of God, and he concluded: "In all things I gave you an example, how that so labouring ye ought to help the weak, and to remember the words of the Lord Jesus, how he himself said, It is more blessed to give than to receive" (Acts 20:35).

# VII

## A Missionary Party at Work

WHEN did Christianity first reach Europe? It is not possible to be certain. Some traveler or soldier who had accepted the good news and was fired by a determination to spread it must have crossed the narrow seas, or returned to Rome itself, before the events we are to trace in this chapter. Shortly before they took place there had been an expulsion of Jews from Rome, and the historian Suetonius says that this was occasioned by persistent tumults in the Jewish quarter "at the instigation of Chrestus." This word means "a good fellow" and was sometimes used by pagans in their allusions to Christianity and its Founder, to whom the word "Christos" would be an extremely puzzling one. Sanday and Headlam concluded: "There is at least a considerable possibility, not to say probability, that in this enigmatic guise we have an allusion to the effect of the early preaching of Christianity." [1] This preaching usually produced a riot in the Jewish quarter! What we are now concerned with is the first *recorded* mission in Europe. It is to be dated from the autumn of the year

[1] *The International Critical Commentary on Romans*, p. xxi.

50 to the summer of the year 51—though, of course, the actual missionary journey lasted beyond that date. It is about twenty years after the Crucifixion. To the people of the day, however, this entry into Europe would not appear so significant as to us, for whom history has sharply marked the divisions between the continents. It was merely crossing over from one province of the empire to another.

And they went through the region of Phrygia and Galatia, having been forbidden of the Holy Ghost to speak the word in Asia; and when they were come over against Mysia, they assayed to go into Bithynia; and the Spirit of Jesus suffered them not; and passing by Mysia, they came down to Troas. And a vision appeared to Paul in the night; There was a man of Macedonia standing, beseeching him, and saying, Come over into Macedonia, and help us. And when he had seen the vision, straightway we sought to go forth into Macedonia, concluding that God had called us for to preach the gospel unto them. (Acts 16:6-10.)

Many questions are suggested by this passage. The most obvious are: What does all the geography mean? Who were the people concerned?

The incident is on Paul's second missionary journey, whose origin is described in Acts 15:36-41. The party had worked round by land from Antioch to Tarsus, then north by the Cilician Gates through the Taurus Mountains—in the opposite direction to that taken by Alexander on his advance into Asia. This is still one of the wildest parts of the world; in Paul's days there would not be room for two laden camels to pass each other—

and so it remained until Ibrahim Pasha blasted the rocks in the nineteenth century.

Thus they reached the high island country of Asia Minor and visited churches which Paul had founded earlier, at Derbe, Lystra, Iconium, and Antioch in Pisidia. A period of uncertainty followed. Should they establish themselves in the rich and populous province of Asia, with its great capital Ephesus? Paul must have felt the attraction of such a course, yet it became clear to them that God did not then wish them so much as to preach in Asia. Should they press northeast to Bithynia, bordering upon the Sea of Marmora and the Black Sea? At first that seemed the thing to do; and they began the journey, but "the Spirit of Jesus suffered them not." So they turned back, through Mysia, without preaching there, for it was in the province of Asia, until they came to Troas.

Troas was a comparatively modern city near the ancient Troy. When founded by the successors of Alexander, it was named after him, Alexandreia Troas. Rome—partly no doubt because the family of the Caesars boasted its descent from Aeneas of Troy—raised it to the rank of a colony, and Augustus renamed it Colonia Augusta Alexandreia Troas. But what of the party which had reached this important place?

First there was Paul. He no longer had Barnabas for companion, as on his first journey. For reasons which appeared sufficient to him there had been a separation between the two evangelists, and Barnabas' place was taken by Silas, or Silvanus. This introduces us to an important secondary figure in early Church history. He was associated with Paul in the writing of I and II Thessalonians, and it is fairly certain that he played a considerable part in the writing of I Peter. Peter says that he wrote this through him (I Pet. 5:12). In I Thess. 2:6 Paul speaks of Silas and himself as "apostles of Christ," which may mean that he received an actual commission from Jesus himself. There is a later tradition that he was one of the seventy appointed by Jesus as an outer circle of apostles.

He may well have been one of those "eyewitnesses, and ministers of the word" on whom St. Luke drew for his Gospel (Luke 1:2); and the affinities observable between I Peter and St. Peter's speeches in Acts as well as other parts of the narrative in Acts 1:13, are perhaps to be traced to information which he supplied; all the more as Luke and Silas were for some time fellow-travellers.[2]

He was, like Paul, a Roman citizen. He came with Paul from Jerusalem, after the Council, to Antioch, to deliver the council's decision about Gentile converts. Silas, like his companion Judas, was a prophet; and both of them improved the occasion with long speeches which helped to bring peace to the disturbed Church (Acts 15:22, 30-33). Silas liked the place so much, and was so attracted by Paul, that he stayed behind at Antioch until he was chosen by Paul to be his companion upon the new missionary venture.

A third member had joined the party at Lystra. This

[2] Selwyn, *op. cit.*, pp. 11-12.

was Timothy, a young man who would be very useful in making many of the arrangements of the journey, and who had a certain facility in preaching. Paul came to rely upon him a great deal and was always ready to say what a valuable member of the team he was. His father was a Greek, and his mother a Jewess who had accepted the new faith. It was well known that Timothy was uncircumcised, so, to avoid scandalizing the Jews in the district, the operation was carried through (Acts 16:1-3).

No other members of the party are named. But the presence of a fourth can be inferred from the narrative, and that is the author of the book himself, "Luke, the beloved physician" (Col. 4:14). *"They* came down to Troas," we have read, and a verse later, "straightway *we* sought to go forth into Macedonia, concluding that God had called us for to preach the gospel unto them." This change of pronoun cannot be unintentional; and in Acts there are a number of passages, known as the "we" sections, in which the employment of the first person plural indicates that the author is drawing upon his own diary of the events recorded.[3] Rackham, in his commentary on Acts, rightly draws attention to its author's

modesty or entire self-effacement. . . . There is not a word about his own work, his "praise in the gospel," his services to S. Paul, not even a hint of S. Paul's affection for him.

[3] The *we* appears in 16:10, and the narrative is in the first person until vs. 17. The *we* reappears in 20:6, and the use of the first person is fairly continuous until the end.

And when he cannot help betraying his presence, he does it simply by writing *we* (and not *I*) .[4]

Of Luke himself much has been written. His medical interest and knowledge are apparent from his writing. He would even rally to the defense of his profession when it was attacked, as a comparison between Mark 5:26 and Luke 8:43 makes clear. In the former we read that the woman with the issue of blood "had suffered many things of many physicians, and had spent all that she had, and was nothing bettered but rather grew worse." This was too much even for Luke. He amended the passage to read that she "had spent all her living upon physicians, and could not be healed of any." His interest in the sea becomes apparent at once in his account of the crossing to Europe:

Setting sail therefore from Troas, we made a straight course to Samothrace, and the day following to Neapolis; and from thence to Philippi, which is a city of Macedonia, the first of the district, a Roman colony. (Acts 16:11-12.)

Because Philippi was not really the first city of the district, a title more rightly applied to Amphipolis, some think that Luke was a native of the place whose local patriotism could not be restrained. At any rate the building up of the Church there, after the first converts had been gained by the pioneer missionaries, owed more to Luke than to anyone else.

It is important that Philippi was a Roman colony. It

[4] *Westminster Commentary,* p. xxxii.

was an outpost of Rome, garrisoned by Roman soldiers to restrain the brigand bands from the hinterland and given a cultural mission through the settlement of a number of families of Roman citizens. There were people in Philippi very proud of the fact that their citizenship was in Rome; to the Christians in the city Paul was to write: "Our citizenship is in heaven" (Phil. 3:20).

There were only a few Jews in Philippi; the missionaries found no synagogue anywhere but noticed a fenced plot by the riverside which they took to be a proseuche, or Jewish place of prayer. Jews often worshiped by the waterside because of the considerable part which water played in their services. It was "by the rivers of Babylon" that the exiles wept as they remembered Jerusalem (Ps. 137). The Roman poet Juvenal gave as an instance of the decay of the native religion in the capital that

> The groves and streams which once were sacred ground
> Are now let out to Jews.[5]

When the Sabbath came, the missionaries made their way to the little plot. No great congregation had assembled—only a few women. But they were glad to listen to what these preachers had to say. To one of them their message came with the force of a revelation.

Lydia was a businesswoman in the textile trade, in a fairly big way of business. She came from Thyatira in Asia Minor, where there was a guild of dyers using the purple extracted from a fish in combination with the

[5] *Satires* III. 11-13.

mineral springs in which their district abounded. Lydia must have been an agent for the sale of the garments they had dyed. Her name was that of the district in which Thyatira is situated. This may mean that she was of servile origin; but if so, that had been left behind long ago, and her business ability found a congenial outlet in the Macedonian society, where the emancipation of women was relatively advanced. It is even more important that she is described as "one that worshipped God" (Acts 16:14); she was not a Jewess, but a God-fearer.

As a result of the apostles' preaching Lydia was baptized, with her household. In the ancient world children or dependents naturally followed the head of a family when so momentous a decision was made as a change in religion. Similarly in the early Middle Ages the members of a tribe would mostly follow their leader when he was converted to Christianity. This has its weaknesses, but it also has its strength. It reduces the number of uprooted men and women who are members of the new community and may easily, just because they are uprooted, become dependent upon it for a means of livelihood.

In the early days of missionary work in India converts were baptized singly and alone. They were transplanted into a new life utterly foreign, and some of them proved unsatisfactory. Few missionaries could enter into the intense loneliness of such converts; driven from their old homes, their wives taken from them, abandoned by their friends, forced to find a new social life among people who could hardly understand the psychological storm involved in the change. Converts were brought to Christ one by one, and they still are, for nothing can take the place of personal conversion. But the problem facing a solitary convert is terrible.[6]

For Lydia this was eased by the fact that her dependents accepted the new loyalty when she did. Lydia's house at once became the headquarters for the missionary party; she had room for all of them. Later on it was probably her wealth which made possible the generous gifts which were sent to Paul in Thessalonica and in prison at Rome.

We have already seen the part which magic played in the Hellenistic world. The first convert to Christianity in Europe was a God-fearer. That might have been expected. But the second was a magician, or something very like it. As the missionaries went about the city, they could not fail to realize that they were being followed by a rather strange girl. She was well known in Philippi. She believed herself to be possessed by a divine spirit; some unscrupulous capitalists had got hold of her and were making a pretty penny from her fortunetelling. Her description in the Acts suggests that she had powers of ventriloquism also. Wherever the missionaries went, she went too; and she cried out after them: "These men are servants of the Most High God, which proclaim unto you the way of salvation" (Acts 16:17). In time this became more than Paul could stand. "But Paul, being sore

---

[6] W. Wilson Cash, *The Missionary Church*, pp. 60-61. The same problem faces converts to Christianity in the mass industrial society of the modern West.

troubled, turned and said to the spirit, I charge thee in the name of Jesus Christ to come out of her. And it came out that very hour." (Acts 16:18.)

Paul treated her as inspired, not by God, but by an evil demon. His exorcism was effective. Here was a new member of the Church. But at once her employers began to cause trouble. Their little gold mine was of no use to them any more. These Christian missionaries must be hounded from the place. They laid hold of Paul and Silas by main force, dragged them into the market place, and formally arraigned them before the chief magistrates of the city. Their real grievance was an economic one, that they were out of an income, but they cloaked it in a more respectable dress. They began by raising the dust of anti-Semitism. "What are these Jews doing in our city anyhow?" they asked. To this they added metropolitan pride. "These men, being Jews, do exceedingly trouble our city, and set forth customs which it is not lawful for us to receive, or to observe, being Romans." (Acts 16:20-21.) No doubt the accusers had their hired ruffians in the crowd, and these proceeded to raise an uproar. The duumvirs, or magistrates, were consequently intimidated—here was no impartial Roman justice. They ordered Paul and Silas to be stripped naked and beaten with rods on the spot. It was just the kind of entertainment for which the baser members of the crowd were hoping. Paul and Silas were led away, smarting from their wounds, to the prison.

This cannot have been a very imposing building. Late at night the two missionaries were there, with their feet in stocks, yet singing hymns of praise to God. Then there was an earthquake; the ramshackle place collapsed, and the prisoners found themselves free.[7] In a panic the jailer was about to commit suicide when he heard Paul shouting out: "Do thyself no harm: for we are all here" (Acts 16:28). He called for lights —which would indeed be needed in an earthquake at midnight—"and sprang in, and, trembling for fear, fell down before Paul and Silas, and brought them out, and said, Sirs, what must I do to be saved?" (Acts 16:29-30). No time here for any elaborate instruction; that must come afterward. Yet the beginnings of a creed are to be observed in Paul's reply: "Believe on the Lord Jesus, and thou shalt be saved, thou and thy house" (Acts 16:31). Both he and Silas added a good deal more, but the end was a family baptism. To the Philippian church there were now added the city jailer and his household.

This did not solve every problem. In the morning the magistrates, who during a disturbed night had doubtless thought again about the way in which they had al-

[7] "Any one that has seen a Turkish prison will not wonder that the doors were thrown open: each door was merely closed by a bar, and the earthquake, as it passed along the ground, forced the door posts apart from each other, so that the bar slipped from its hold, and the door swung open. The prisoners were fastened to the wall or in wooden stocks; and the chains and stocks were detached from the wall, which was shaken so the spaces gaped between the stones. In the great earthquakes of 1880 at Smyrna, and 1881 at Scio, I had the opportunity of seeing and hearing of the strangely capricious action of an earthquake, which behaves sometimes like a playful, good-natured sprite, when it spares its full terrors" (W. M. Ramsay, *St. Paul the Traveller and the Roman Citizen,* 19th ed., p. 221).

lowed themselves to be intimidated by a mercantile mob, sent a message that Paul and Silas were to be allowed to go. Paul now played his trump card—the results of which would be of value to the church which he was so shortly to leave behind. He would have them know that neither he nor Silas could be disposed of so easily. "They have beaten us publicly, uncondemned, men that are Romans, and have cast us into prison; and do they now cast us out privily? nay verily; but let them come themselves and bring us out." (Acts 16:37.) The magistrates were terrified. They did come themselves, with an earnest entreaty to the missionaries to move on somewhere else. This they did, but first they met the church at Lydia's house and were given encouragement for their journey. Paul and Silas were joined by Timothy—but Luke was left behind.

Obviously the church needed further teaching; Luke was the man for the job. He may have been there for six years. The Philippian church always remained faithful to Paul. He was always glad to recall its fellowship; whenever he thought of it, it was with joy. The quality of its life must have been derived in no small measure from the fact that it had Luke to nurture it.

For the three missionaries it was out of the frying pan into the fire. When they reached Thessalonica, they found a Jewish synagogue. Paul spoke here on three successive Sabbath days, maintaining his gospel, so amazing to the Jews, "that it behoved the Christ to suffer, and to rise again from the dead; and that this Jesus, whom, said he, I proclaim unto you, is the Christ" (Acts

17:3) . This was done with constant reference to the Hebrew Scriptures, no doubt especially to those Servant Songs in the book of Isaiah in which Christian imagination has traced the very lineaments of the Messiah. Luke's summary makes it clear that it was the same apostolic *kerygma* which was being proclaimed by the apostles. Nor was their preaching unsuccessful. Of the Jews "some were persuaded." The God-fearers heard the message much more readily; "of the devout Greeks a great multitude" were persuaded. Many of the wives of the principal men in the city even cast in their lot with Paul and Silas. We are not told what Timothy was doing, but it is made clear that Silas had an important part to play.

At Thessalonica it seems that St. Paul did most of the public preaching; but Silvanus (as we will now call him) was at least equally to the fore in gathering in the converts, especially among the leading society women who found his charm and polish more attractive perhaps than the ruggedness of St. Paul.[8]

Yet even as they preached and argued, and won such apparent success, opposition was hardening against them. There were men in the synagogue who knew Paul's past, who despised him as a renegade, and who felt the urgent necessity of putting a stop to the preaching of this Way before it was too late. Where arguments failed, brute force must be employed. They got hold of another set of ruffians—"certain lewd fellows of the

[8] Selwyn, *op. cit.*, p. 13. I Thessalonians makes it clear that the mission lasted more than three weeks.

baser sort" is the attractive translation in the King James Version—to attack the house of Jason, with whom the apostles were staying. Jason and some of the other Christians were dragged before the city authorities and accused of giving hospitality to troublemakers from outside. "These that have turned the world upside down are come hither also"—here was no commendation, but a declaration that these Christian preachers were dangerous revolutionaries, stirring up trouble wherever they went. Thessalonica had political privileges it did not wish to lose. There had been riots in Jerusalem and Galatia and Philippi; there had been the riot about "Chrestus" in Rome. Once passions had been inflamed in Thessalonica, it was easy to claim that these men should be suppressed. As he wrote his record, from the account which the others gave him, Luke may well have remembered the accusation brought against Jesus himself: "We found this man perverting our nation, and forbidding to give tribute to Caesar, and saying that he himself is Christ a king" (23:2). The same things are now said of his followers: "These all act contrary to the decrees of Caesar, saying that there is another king, one Jesus" (Acts 17:7). It was an accusation which was often to be repeated, and in the end it was the refusal to put Caesar before Christ which brought about the long persecution of Christianity.

The suggestion of treason put both the authorities and the crowd into a panic. Jason, who may well have been a citizen of some importance, had to pay bail before he got away. Paul and Silas slipped away by night to Berea, where Timothy joined them later. Here, again, they made for the synagogue, and this time were encouraged by a much more favorable reception. The members paid courteous attention, and there was much looking up of biblical references to see whether Paul's arguments were well grounded. The result was that not only some, but many, of the Jews were persuaded; there was a marked success in the circles of God-fearers and among the leading women of the community. All was going well until a party of Jews came from Thessalonica to stir up fresh trouble. Again Paul had to move on, heading for Athens, where Silas and Timothy were shortly to join him.

"Come over into Macedonia, and help us!" Macedonia did not seem to have much of a welcome for the Christian missionaries. Wherever they went there were accusations, riots, the risk of eventual bloodshed. Yet the extent and virulence of the opposition are a measure of the effectiveness of the preaching. No wonder the synagogue members in Thessalonica were stirred when they found that Paul and Silas were stealing away their best and richest supporters. They were revolted even more deeply by what seemed to them to be the specious brilliance of Paul's arguments, the dangerous heresies which he was propounding. To them the preaching of the Cross was indeed a stumbling block. Yet the church grew. Nor was it made up only of the lower elements in the population. Luke tells us how ready some of the leading Gentile women, already attracted by the Law and the Prophets, were to accept the preaching of this

*103*

one in whom Law and Prophets found their fulfillment. The missionaries moved on, but they left behind them groups of Christians, meeting in the most suitable houses, joining in worship on the Sabbath, and on Sunday, and on other days as well. It was to such groups that a number of the epistles of Paul were written. It was to meet their needs that, in the end, the Gospels themselves were composed.

# VIII

## A Missionary Letter

CHURCHES had been founded, then left suddenly and hurriedly behind. In Thessalonica, Paul and his companions must have wondered how things were going in Philippi. They were not overworried because Luke had been left in charge, and they were swiftly encouraged by two contributions to the expenses of the missionary campaign which their friends at Philippi sent them (Phil. 4:16). After they had escaped by night from Thessalonica, they must have wondered a good deal about the church established there, on the face of it much stronger than the one at Philippi, but young and beset by enemies. The Christians they had left behind must also have wondered about the missionaries who had brought them to Christ: "How are they faring? Has Paul managed to keep out of prison? How good it would be to hear from them! If only they were here to answer some of the difficult questions which have arisen since they left!"

It was a fortunate circumstance that correspondence was fairly easy in the Roman Empire. One reason for the creation and maintenance of the straight, hard

Roman roads was that there should be frequent and rapid communication between the imperial headquarters and the provinces. What served the government served the trader and the private individual as well. And it served the growing Church. Messengers were available; papyrus for letters was not expensive. A considerable correspondence went on. Its legacy to us is contained in the epistles in the New Testament.

From Berea, Paul went on to Athens and then to Corinth. At Athens he was joined by Timothy. He was delighted to see him, to have his service and companionship once more. Yet the needs of the Church came before personal convenience. As the two of them talked together, the thought of Thessalonica came up again and again. In the end it was decided that Timothy should return there to find out what was happening.

And so at length, when the separation became intolerable, we thought the best plan was for me to stay at Athens alone, while Timothy, our brother and fellow-worker in the Gospel of Christ, was sent to strengthen and encourage you in your faith. We did not want any of you to lose heart at the troubles you were going through, but to realise that we Christians must expect such things. Actually we did warn you what to expect, when we were with you, and our words have come true, as you know. (I Thess. 3:1-4.) [1]

Timothy returned with good news:

With a glowing account of your faith and love, and definite news that you cherish happy memories of us and long

[1] J. B. Phillips, *Letters to Young Churches*. Copyright 1947 by the Macmillan Co., and used by their permission.

to see us as much as we to see you—how these things have cheered us in all the miseries and troubles we ourselves are going through. (3:6-7.) [2]

The Thessalonians had faced the season of testing well.

You thus became examples to all who believe in Macedonia and Achaia. You have become a sort of sounding-board from which the word of the Lord has rung out, not only in Macedonia and Achaia but everywhere where the story of your faith in God has become known. We find we don't have to tell people about it. They tell *us* the story of our coming to you: how you turned from idols to serve the true living God. (1:7-9.) [3]

Nevertheless weaknesses required attention. People were saying—Jews probably—that the apostles had no real status in the Church; that they were free lances, out for their own ends. These charges had to be met (I Thess. 2:1-12). Nor were all the converts living by the high moral standards which the missionaries had enjoined. In a great city where to be a Christian meant to be cut off from much social intercourse, it was not surprising that the attractions of the old life were still felt by some. They had to be reminded of the direct moral teaching which they had been given (I Thess. 4:1-12). When the missionaries were with them, they had spoken a good deal about the coming End of the Age. Since then some Christians had died, and the others were curious about their fate (I Thess. 4:13–5:11). The discipline of the Church also needed to be stiffened, and the hands strengthened of those who had been left in charge (I Thess. 5:12-13).

When this was reported by Timothy in Corinth, the three missionaries dictated the letter which begins: "Paul, and Silvanus, and Timothy, unto the church of the Thessalonians in God the Father, and the Lord Jesus Christ: Grace to you and peace." It is known to us as I Thessalonians. It was a genuine letter, cast into the usual letter form of the time, a form now, as it were, baptized into Christ. No doubt the thought and expression were largely Paul's; the second letter to the same church, which opens in almost exactly the same way, concludes with his personal signature (3:17). We can imagine with what excitement, with what nods of approval and meaningful glances across the room, it must first have been read out at a gathering of the church, perhaps in Jason's house. Yet even those eager hearers could not have guessed how historic was the occasion at which they were assisting.

Many scholars think that the Epistle to the Galatians had been written earlier; apart from that possibility I Thessalonians is our first New Testament book. Other letters followed. A second letter to Thessalonica itself dealt with the too-great excitement about the End of the Age which was possessing a number of the Christians. The successful mission in Corinth occasioned a correspondence which has already proved valuable in our endeavor to elucidate the original missionary message, and which illuminates vividly the life of the Christian

Church in the degraded cities of the Greco-Roman world. It was to cities that the Christian message was directed by these evangelists; a strategic plan was forming in Paul's mind, leading to Rome and beyond Rome. It was to the church in the imperial city that he wrote his most carefully considered and magisterial statement of Christian doctrine, so that there should be no mistaking the gospel for which he stood. Yet even when he wrote to Rome there was no escaping the native Palestinian note in the Christianity which he preached. "For ye received not the spirit of bondage again unto fear," he wrote, recalling the Roman Christians to the experience of their conversion, "but ye received the spirit of adoption, whereby we cry, Abba, Father" (8:15). "Abba" is not Greek but Aramaic. It is the word for father which Jesus himself must have used.

There is no space in this short account to tell the story of the continuing Christian mission in the intervals of which these letters were written. We may note in passing that Paul found in what nowadays we are learning to call interchurch aid the sovereign remedy for divisions between the churches. He used all his energies and persuasiveness to encourage the richer Gentile churches to raise funds and gifts in kind for their necessitous fellow Christians in Palestine. A large section of II Corinthians is concerned with this practical matter (chs. 8 and 9). He was a skillful money-raiser. He told the Macedonians how well the Greeks in Achaia were doing, and then wrote to Corinth to tell the Christians there that they must hurry if they were not to be beaten by Macedonia:

Indeed I have told the Macedonians with some pride that "Achaia was ready to undertake this service a twelvemonth ago." Your enthusiasm has consequently been a stimulus to many of them. I am, however, sending the brothers just to make sure that our pride in you is not unjustified. For, between ourselves, it would never do if some of the Macedonians were to accompany me on my visit to you and find you unprepared for this act of generosity! We (not to speak of you) should be horribly ashamed, just because we had been so proud and confident of you. This is my reason, then, for urging the brothers to visit you before I come myself, so that they can get your promised gift ready in time. (II Cor. 9:2-5.) [4]

There would be no resisting this appeal, and it may be that the Department of Reconstruction and Inter-Church Aid of the World Council of Churches wishes that it had a Paul on its staff for the furtherance of a campaign which has such marked similarities with his own.

It was at the conclusion of this task that the presence of Paul in the temple at Jerusalem occasioned a riot and his arrest and imprisonment in Caesarea, the first stage in the long and hazardous journey which was to bring him, a prisoner, to Rome. He had, of course, been a prisoner several times before, and there are those who think that the "captivity epistles"—Ephesians, Philippians, Colossians, and Philemon—were written during an earlier imprisonment, only hinted at in the book of Acts, in Ephesus. (Ephesians itself is almost certainly a circular

[4] J. B. Phillips, *Letters to Young Churches.* Copyright 1947 by the Macmillan Co., and used by their permission.

letter to the churches of Asia Minor, rather than a letter to the church in Ephesus.) But there do not seem to be convincing reasons for giving up the earlier belief that these were written during his imprisonment in Rome.

Of this imprisonment his old friends in Philippi had heard with deep distress. What could they do to help him? They could send him money, as they had done in the early days, but could they not do more? After discussion they agreed to send, not only money, but one of themselves, a young man called Epaphroditus, to do for Paul all that they themselves would have wished to do. Epaphroditus joined the apostle in Rome. At once he started doing things to help him and in the end worked so hard that he fell ill and was in danger of dying. When he recovered, Paul noticed that he was not his old cheerful self. "What is wrong?" he asked.

"I am very worried about the people at home," he said. "They've heard that I am ill—and they haven't heard that I have recovered. The rumor is probably going round that I am already dead."

To which Paul replied: "That gives me the opportunity I have been waiting for. I have wanted for very long to send my friends in Philippi a letter of encouragement. There are none that mean more to me. Besides there are those two women who have quarreled. I must see if I can bring them together again. You must take it back. I shall make it very clear to them that you have not failed in the task they set you. You had better begin to make preparations for travel."

So he dictated what we call the Epistle to the Philip-

pians. The whole of it should be read straight through—
in the version of F. A. Cockin, Bishop of Bristol. This
may well be studied later alongside the version of 1881.
But a modern translation in ordinary speech is a fitting
reminder that Paul wrote for a modern situation, in language which most of the ordinary people in the church
would be able to follow. There they were—Lydia, the
girl who had been set in her right mind after being ex-
ploited, the governor of the jail, and other nameless
Christians. What has Paul to say to them? If what follows
is read aloud to a group of fellow Christians, they may
recapture something of the feeling of the early Church.

1:1-2. Greeting from Paul and Timothy, two of Christ's
bondmen, to all the Christians in Philippi, and to the
leaders of the Church. We wish you grace and peace from
God our Father, and from our Lord Jesus Christ.

3-11. I thank God whenever I think of you; and my
prayers for you are always full of happiness, as I remember
how you took your full share in the work of spreading the
Good News, from the very first. I know that He who has
begun this good work in you will go on completing it until
the time when Christ comes into His own. I could not
think otherwise of you, when one of my dearest memories is
the way in which you have all shared in the grace which
has enabled me to face imprisonment, and to stand firm in
my defence of the Gospel. God knows how much I love
and long for you, with something of Christ's own love. And
my prayer for you is that your love may grow and deepen,
bringing you the knowledge and spiritual insight which can
discern the things which really matter: so may Christ find
you sincere and upright, able to offer Him a rich harvest

of the goodness which really comes from Him. The glory of it will be God's not yours.

12-18. I should like you to know that all my affairs have been turning out to the advancement of Christ's cause. All Caesar's Guards and the palace servants know that I am a prisoner because I am a Christian, and the very fact of my imprisonment has given fresh courage to my fellow-Christians to speak out more boldly. Some, it is true, are preaching Christ with the mean motive of trying to make things worse for me: but others do it out of goodwill, because they know that it is for the sake of the Gospel that I lie in bonds. What does it all come to? Why only that, one way or another, honestly or dishonestly, Christ gets preached. And that is more than enough to make me glad.

19-26. I know that it will all come out right for me, for you are praying, and Christ supplies the help of His Spirit. All that I really care for is that I may never be ashamed, but may put Christ first, now as ever, whether in life or death. For to me life means Christ, and death means gain: and yet to go on living means more fruitful work. So I am in a dilemma, and hardly know which to choose. I long to go to join my Lord, which is far better. But for your sakes I ought to go on living. And so I feel sure that I shall be spared to carry you a stage further in the joyful progress of your faith. I shall come back to you, and my return will give you still more reason for rejoicing in all that Christ means to you.

27-30. Only remember that you must live a life worthy of Christ's Gospel. Then, whether I come and see you, or only hear of you from a distance, I shall know that you are standing shoulder to shoulder, putting up a good fight for the faith. If you never let your enemies succeed in frightening you, that will show them that they are done for, and that you are triumphant, because you are on God's side. You have been given the great honour, not only of believing in Christ, but also of being allowed to suffer for His sake: you are fighting the same battle, which, as once you saw, and now you hear, I am fighting myself.

2:1-11. I appeal to you by all that you hold dear, by all the strength and love you find in Christ, by the unity which His Spirit gives you, by your own affection for me, let me have the supreme joy of knowing that you are living in harmony, really loving one another, working as a team. Keep clear of envy and vanity: have the humility to put others higher than yourselves: have an eye for others' needs and interests, not only for your own. The spirit that you need is the spirit that you see in Jesus Christ. Though He was divine by nature, He did not count equality with God as something to be grasped at, but emptied Himself and took the nature of a servant. Made a man like us, and sharing our human nature, He humbled Himself in His obedience even to the point of death, and death on a cross. Therefore God raised Him to the highest honour, and gave Him the name which is above all other names, that everything in creation should bow before the name of Jesus, and every tongue confess that He alone is Lord, to God's praise and glory.

12-18. So, beloved friends, who have always listened to me, not only when I was with you, but now also in my absence, keep on working away at your salvation, with a true sense of all that is at stake, remembering that all that you desire and achieve is just God's goodness working in you. In all that you do avoid complaints, and captious questioning (of God's goodness). So will you be innocent and sincere, living like true sons of God in a world which has all gone wrong. As your master said, "Let your light shine before men," and bring to them a message that has life in it. Then, indeed, I shall rejoice in Christ's presence, to think that I have not run or worked for nothing. Even if I have to give my life as a sacrifice for the faith which you are offering to

God, I shall rejoice with you over it, and expect you to rejoice with me.

19-30. I hope, if it is Christ's will, to be able soon to send Timothy to visit you, that I may have the refreshment of hearing news of you. I know nobody who has the same genuine concern for all your affairs as he has. So many care only for their own interests, not for those of Christ. But you know how he has proved himself, rendering me a real son's service in the preaching of the Gospel. So at any rate I hope to send him as soon as I can see what is going to happen to me: and I trust that I may be able to come myself before very long. Meanwhile, I felt that I must send Epaphroditus, who has been a brother to me, a real comrade in the work and warfare, and the bringer of your contribution to my needs. He has been pining to see you, and really distressed since he knew that you had heard about his illness. And indeed, he was ill, nearly dying. But God had mercy on him, and on me too, and spared me from grief on grief. So I am all the more anxious to send him, that you may be reassured by the sight of him, and that my own mind may be more at rest. I know that you will give him a joyful welcome. Value men like that; for he risked his life in Christ's service, by trying to make up for the help that you would all have given me.

3:1. Finally, brothers, may Christ give you joy. I am never tired of saying that word "joy" to you; and it does you no harm to hear it more than once.

2-6. But beware of those crafty mischief-makers, the die-hard, orthodox party. We have got all the orthodoxy that matters, we who worship God in spirit, and put our trust in Christ alone, and not in natural advantages. Not that I could not boast a pretty list of natural advantages if I cared to. Received into the Jewish Church on the proper day, a member of the chosen race, and of the favoured tribe, sprung from good Hebrew stock, brought up in the strictest observance of the Law, going out of my way to persecute the Christians, a model of the goodness which the Law prescribes.

7-16. But all these "advantages" of mine I counted just dead loss for Christ's sake. Aye, and I count everything dead loss compared to the one thing that matters, the knowledge of Jesus Christ my Lord. For His sake I let them all go—they were nothing but refuse—that I might win Christ and belong to Him. The only kind of goodness that I want is not the kind that comes from law-keeping, but that which comes from trusting Christ, the goodness which Christ gives to those who will so trust. I want to know Him, to share the power that brought Him through death to life, to share His sufferings, dying as He died, in the hope that so I may win through to the life that He now lives. It is not that I have already attained, or reached the level of perfection; but I press on in the hope that I may lay hold of it, as I have been already laid hold of by Jesus Christ. I do not reckon myself as one who has already laid hold of it: but there is just one thing that I do. Putting the past behind me, and reaching out to that which lies ahead, I race towards the post for the prize which waits for those whom God has called to follow Christ. This then must be the aim for all of us who are full grown; and if there are any who cannot yet see it, God will make that also plain in His own time. Only we must try to live by the guidance which has been already given us.

17-21; 4:1. Follow my example—and not mine only but that of all those whose life is moulded on mine. For alas! there are many, of whom I have often warned you, and now do so again with deep distress, who are real enemies of all that Christ's cross stands for. They are heading for ruin: they make a god out of their own gross appetites: they glory in their shame: they are earthly minded. We live as citizens of another world, the world to which we look for the coming of our Saviour Jesus Christ, who will transform this life of humiliation into the glorious life in which He lives, by the same power by which He can bring all things to own His sway. So then, my friends, whom I love and long for, source of my joy and crown of all my labours, stand fast in this faith, as Christians ought to do.

2-3. I would beg my two friends who have quarrelled to be reconciled again to one another, as Christ would have them be. And I ask you, faithful fellow-worker, to give them all the help which they deserve as women who have toiled and struggled at my side for the cause of the Gospel.

4-7. My last word to you is "Joy," and I repeat it once again. Be known to all men for your courteous forbearance. You have not long to wait: Christ's time is coming soon. Have no anxieties, but simply tell God what you want in prayer, and thank Him for what He has already given you. And His peace, the peace which is far better than all our careful planning, will garrison your hearts and minds with Christ's own guard.

8-9. One word more—Fill your minds with everything true, and noble, and upright, and pure, everything lovely and attractive, all excellence, all that deserves praise. Store it all up and meditate upon it. Put into practice what I have tried to teach you, what you have heard me say, and seen me do. And God, whose gift is peace, will be with you.

10-20. It means so much to me that once again you should have made the effort to provide for my needs. You have, I know, thought of it before, but lacked the opportunity to put it into practice. Please do not think that I am speaking as though I had been in want because of your neglect. I have learnt how to be content in any circumstances: I know how to do with little, and how to enjoy abundance. I possess the secret of all kinds of life, plenty or hunger, prosperity or want. I can face them all because I do not rely on my own strength. But, none the less, it was good of you to help me in my time of need. And you know that I am glad to take your help; for you remember that in the early days it was you alone of all the churches that I allowed to help me in the matter of money: you even sent me contributions after I had left you, more than once. It is not the gifts that I covet, it is the record of good deeds which God puts down to your account. Now I have all I need and more, since Epaphroditus came, bringing your latest gift, a precious offering, the kind of sacrifice that God really values. I cannot meet your needs in return, but God will, for He has everything to give in Christ. Glory to Him, now and always, Amen.

21-23. Give my love to all the Christians in Philippi. All my friends here send their love, and all the Christians, specially those in the imperial household. May the gracious power and love of Christ fill your hearts. Good-bye.

# IX

## Hymns, Creeds, and Catechisms

THE Epistle to the Philippians is a lively personal letter, full of intimate touches, as might be expected in one written by a missionary to a church with which his relations had been particularly close. The letter was dictated in reply to one which the Philippians had sent. Paul takes up the points which they have made, telling them, for example, not to be depressed because he was in prison; certainly he was chained by the wrist to a Roman soldier every day, but this was a heaven-sent missionary opportunity! Sometimes indeed he was depressed by those who were preaching Christ, yet felt that the interpretation of the faith for which he stood was wrong, and did their best to make his bonds more irksome to him. Well, at any rate, Christ was being preached. There are the digressions one might expect in a dictated letter—perhaps occasioned by the arrival of fresh news or by more normal interruptions. All his courteous tact comes out in writing of Epaphroditus; but he seems overanxious to press the claims of Timothy for consideration, and at the end he has a most awkward way of saying "Thank you" for the gifts which Epaphroditus had brought. Here too we find Paul the psychologist telling his friends to let their minds dwell upon the really important things—even when they belonged to their old pagan life, if they were worthy. (This seems to be the implication of what the Revised Version renders in 4:8: "If there be any virtue, and if there be any praise.") There is a straight word for Euodia and Syntyche—and a hard task for the person whom he refers to as "true yokefellow," who is charged to bring these women workers together again (4:2-3).

There is, of course, far more in the epistle than this. Its heart is in the aspiration: "That I may know him, and the power of his resurrection, and the fellowship of his sufferings, becoming conformed unto his death; if by any means I may attain unto the resurrection from the dead" (3:10-11). His spiritual biography is here also, with its revolutionary climax: "What things were gain to me, these have I counted loss for Christ" (3:7). There appears at one point a part of the blessing which has concluded Holy Communion services for hundreds of years (4:7). A modern translation is a reminder that the word rendered "keep" is one normally used of a sentry on guard. Here is a sentence from Scripture which through frequent repetition has become a part of our common heritage. In the life of the early Church the reverse process also took place. Well-known sentences found their place in writings which a later generation was to recognize as Scripture. Sometimes it is only a phrase or a word. Paul could use the Aramaic "Abba" in writing to the church at Rome because it was already familiar in its worship—as "Hallelujah" and "Hosanna" still are in ours. All over the Roman Empire men and women, non-Jews, found themselves echoing prayers with the Hebrew ejaculation "Amen."

Sometimes more than a sentence was quoted. The very great passage in Philippians (2:5-11) where Paul sets out the meaning of the Incarnation is composed of carefully balanced sentences culminating in a dramatic doxology, and is poetry rather than prose. Some writers have suggested that he was using a hymn already in existence; if so, the early Church had an unknown poet worthy to be compared with the unknown one who wrote the Servant Songs in the book of Isaiah. Praise and thanksgiving played a great part in the worship of the early Church; was not its principal service often called the Eucharist, or "Thanksgiving"? In Ephesians we read of "speaking one to another in psalms and hymns and spiritual songs, singing and making melody with your heart to the Lord; giving thanks always" (5:19-20). Material for this joyful exercise was already available in the book of Psalms, which the Christian Church at once made its own, charging them with a new and deeper meaning. But the Church had its poets too, one of whom had been quoted in Ephesians a few verses earlier:

> Awake, O sleeper,
> From thy grave arise.
> The light of Christ upon thee shines.
> (5:14.) [1]

---

[1] The translation is that by Dr. J. W. C. Wand, Bishop of London, in *The New Testament Letters*, p. 120.

These are, perhaps, the opening words of a hymn sung at baptism; if so, the readers of the epistle would recognize them at once and recall the moment of their own farewell to the past and entry into new life in a new community.

The two epistles to Timothy and the epistle to Titus —commonly called the Pastoral Epistles—are not considered by most scholars to be the actual work of Paul, though they may contain some material from his hand. They represent, rather, the Church of the middle of the second century, the Church for which the Gospels had already been written. They belong to the age of quotation rather than of immediate experience; a new phrase, "Faithful is the saying," is found in all three. Some of these quotations are in verse. In II Tim. 2:11-13 is what appears to be a hymn on the glories of martyrdom; its verse structure is made clear by Dr. Wand's translation:

> Die we with Christ,
>   And we shall live with Him:
> Endure all,
>   And with Him we shall reign.
>
> Deny we Him,
>   Ourselves shall be denied—
> But seek His love
>   'Twill hold in spite of all.
>
> Dim though our faith,
>   The Christ will faithful prove.
> We are in Him:
>   Himself He cannot fail.[2]

[2] *Ibid.,* p. 147.

It hardly needs to be added that poetry—poetry which could be remembered and repeated, which would give encouragement in dark hours—plays a considerable part in the book of Revelation.

Vague hymns are a modern invention. It is not possible to continue praising for very long without becoming explicit. These early hymns were dogmatic and direct. One in I Tim. 3:16 is half hymn, half creed: "He who was manifested in the flesh, justified in the spirit, seen of angels, preached among the nations, believed on in the world, received up in glory." Were ever a few verses more packed with theology than Phil. 2:5-11? Profession and praise come very close together. As T. R. Glover once said:

In doxology we come nearer to fact than in dogma, for it is out of doxology that historically dogma has grown. The primitive Christian went through an experience; then he broke out in thanksgiving and doxology for it; and finally he, and other people, began to speculate on the relation of the experience so stated to the general sum of human experience and knowledge; and the result of this speculation was called, in the language of the day, dogma.[3]

The historical creeds of the Church arose in time for two main reasons: as baptismal formulas, beliefs accepted by the convert upon his entering the new community; and as a means for the exclusion of error. These needs are both apparent in the New Testament; there, too, is to be found the beginning of creedal forms to meet

[3] *The Christian Tradition and Its Verification*, p. 116.

them. "What must I do to be saved?" cried the Philippian jailer; and the missionaries replied, "Believe on the Lord Jesus, and thou shalt be saved, thou and thy house" (Acts 16:31). In Acts, chapter 8, is the story of the Ethiopian eunuch. "What doth hinder me to be baptized?" he asked—and in the Revised Version, Philip's answer is removed to the margin, because it is not to be found in all the most reliable manuscripts. But some read: "And Philip said, If thou believest with all thy heart, thou mayest. And he answered and said, I believe that Jesus Christ is the Son of God" (vs. 37). If this verse has been interpolated by an early Christian scribe, it may be because that was exactly what he himself had to confess when he became a Christian. What was asked of the believer in early days was simple. He was either for or against; either he accepted the revelation of God in Jesus Christ, or he did not. Baptism was the prelude to the much fuller instruction which followed. In the second century this was changed. There was a long catechumenate—a period of instruction and testing—before baptism actually took place. One reason for this new safeguard was the development of heresy.

Of heresy also there are hints in the New Testament. We remember the background of rival faiths in which the Church's mission was set. It is not surprising that some of these affected some Christian believers. Some were anxious to come to terms with the "new thought" of the time and the "spiritual" ideas of the devotees of the mystery religions. These people were severely trounced by Paul in Col. 2:8-10:

Be careful that nobody spoils your faith, through intellectualism or high-sounding nonsense. Such stuff is at best founded on men's ideas of the nature of the world and disregards Christ! Yet it is in Him that God gives a full and complete expression of Himself (within the physical limits that He set Himself in Christ). Moreover, your own completeness is only realised in Him, Who is the Authority over all authorities, and the Supreme Power over all powers.[4]

In the Revelation people with similar ideas are reprehended as the sect of the Nicolaitans. Generally, they refused to believe that God's world was a good world. Matter for them was evil. If Jesus was indeed the revelation of God, he could never really have become a man. They could not face what Paul accepted from the first, that Jesus was "born of a woman" (Gal. 4:4), that he "died . . . ; and that he was buried" (I Cor. 15:3-4). All this must be spiritualized. Not so, replied the author of the Fourth Gospel: "The word became flesh."

*Flesh*—not, some thought, a very spiritual word; and it was a word which for Paul was almost synonymous with evil. In the Johannine writings, however, it is used to combat this loathed heretical thinking. "Every spirit which confesseth that Jesus Christ is come in the flesh is of God." (I John 4:2.) "For many deceivers are gone forth into the world, even they that confess not that Jesus Christ cometh in the flesh. This is the deceiver and the antichrist." (II John 7.) There is plain speaking here; great things were at stake. The same creedal form

[4] J. B. Phillips, *Letters to Young Churches*. Copyright 1947 by the Macmillan Co., and used by their permission.

125

is found again in I John: "Who is the liar but he that denieth that Jesus is the Christ? This is the antichrist, even he that denieth the Father and the Son. Whosoever denieth the Son, the same hath not the Father: he that confesseth the Son hath the Father also" (2:22-23). In Paul's correspondence there may also be traced the same beginnings of a creed: "If thou shalt confess with thy mouth Jesus as Lord, and shalt believe in thy heart that God raised him from the dead, thou shalt be saved" (Rom. 10:9). "Wherefore I give you to understand, that no man speaking in the Spirit of God saith, Jesus is anathema; and no man can say, Jesus is Lord, but in the Holy Spirit" (I Cor. 12:3). Lord was the new name given to Jesus in Phil. 2:11. The title is applied to him more than 250 times in Paul's epistles. It was, of course, a name frequently used in the mystery religions. "There are gods many, and lords many," he wrote to the Corinthians when discussing the practical issue confronting the Christian housewife that the meat on sale in the Corinthian markets had usually been previously offered before an idol, "yet to us there is one God, the Father, of whom are all things, and we unto him; and one Lord, Jesus Christ, through whom are all things, and we unto him" (8:5-6). Yet the meaning of the word for Paul was not derived from these cults, but from the Hebrew Scriptures. It was a very bold thing to say that the new title given by God to Jesus was Lord, because in the Greek translation of the Old Testament this is consistently used in place of the Hebrew name for God himself, Yahweh. That the idea was Hebrew rather than

Greek is made even clearer by the fact that Paul uses the Aramaic words *Maran atha,* "Our Lord has come!" at the close of I Corinthians (16:22) .[5]

In this chapter and in the next we are pressing back to the spoken word behind the written word, to the spoken word which was active in the life of the Church. Are we therefore in a realm where nothing can be certain? Already we have had sufficient facts to disprove this. When Paul recalled the Corinthians to what he had taught them, it was to what he had himself been taught four or five years after the Crucifixion—and if he was told these things first by disciples in Damascus, they must also have been approved by Peter and James in Jerusalem. There are four factors to be borne in mind in estimating the value of this oral tradition.

First, we must remember that *the first century had no printing, no radio, no motion pictures, no telephone.* Memories did not have so much to compete with as memories have today. Even now it is the testimony of travelers that in the East memories are more retentive than in the industrial West. It is not too much to assume that the early Christians had good memories. They regarded what they had been taught—or what they had themselves experienced—of Christ as the most important knowledge they could ever possess; in their memories these recollections had priority over all others.

Secondly, *they had been trained to use their memories.* The basis of most education, until the twentieth century,

<hr>

[5] The King James Version, which links *Maran atha* with the imprecation which precedes it, makes nonsense of the passage.

was learning by heart. Of course there was too much of this, but it may be questioned whether today the reaction from it has not gone too far. "I was made to learn dates and poetry by heart," writes Dr. G. M. Trevelyan in his *Autobiography,* "as all children ought to be while their memory is still good and retentive, instead of being stuffed with generalizations about history and criticisms of literature which mean nothing to their empty young minds." In the Jewish synagogue—and in a Greek school also—he would probably have been obliged to learn by heart even more. Writes Dr. Paul Levertoff:

As soon as they had mastered the alphabet they received little parchment rolls, specially prepared for school purposes, which contained these passages: (1) Lev. i.-viii. (concerning sacrifices and priesthood); (2) Gen. i.-vi. (Creation, etc.); (3) Dt. vi.4-9 (Divine Unity); Ps. cxiii.-cxviii.; and Num. i.-xi. These excerpts were usually copied by the more advanced pupils as a form of exercise. The first Bible lessons began with Leviticus, probably because in Jerusalem the children of the priests had to be instructed in sacrificial lore; which custom spread to other schools. It must be remembered that the reading of the above passages involved the ability to chant the verses in traditional fashion and to translate them into the Aramaic vernacular. The teacher recited the Bible verses and the pupils repeated them again and again, until they knew both the proper reading of the original and its meaning. Some rabbis considered it permissible for the teacher to divide each verse into small portions. Others again looked upon this method with disfavour.[6]

[6] "The Jewish Elementary School in the First Century A.D.," in *The Teachers' Commentary,* p. 257.

In our Lord's controversies with the Pharisees, as in much of his teaching of the common people, he could assume their familiarity with the Scriptures to which he referred. Their education explains this. Is it possible that Christians who knew Leviticus so well would not treasure with equal tenacity the teaching of their Master?

A third point to be recalled is that for the ancient world *the written was not so important as the spoken word.* "We moderns contrast documentary evidence with hearsay, mere hearsay," wrote Dr. James Moffatt. "No such antithesis prevailed as traditions rose to power in Islam or in Judaism." Islam is regarded pre-eminently as the religion of a book, yet "during the early centuries of Islam there was indeed sharp controversy over the question whether traditions ought to be written at all, with the possible exception of such memoranda as the companions of Muhammad had drawn up." The same held good of Judaism. "The 'customs which Moses delivered us' and which St. Stephen was charged with altering, the 'traditions of my fathers,' for which the apostle Paul had been so zealous, were still unwritten regulations of the Pharisees" until after the fall of Jerusalem. Again:

For the Greek thinkers it is the oral, not the written, word which imparts a throb of life. One has only to read a dialogue like the *Phaedrus* or even the seventh of the epistles in order to understand how a distinguished modern scholar concludes that "Plato does not believe in books for serious purposes." His own writings have proved to be creative literature, but he had no faith in creative literature for the purpose of influence or education. He had no idea of the power possessed by a classic to stir fresh vision. He believed in hearers rather than in readers, and in hearers who were more than mere listeners.[7]

These statements form a significant comment upon the famous statement of Papias, recalling the times when the companions of the apostles were still alive:

On any occasion when a person came who had been a follower of the Elders, I would enquire about the discourses of the Elders—what was said by Andrew, or by Peter, or by Philip, or by Thomas or James, or by John or Matthew or any other of the Lord's disciples, and what Aristion and the Elder John, the disciples of the Lord, say. *For I did not think that I could get so much profit from the contents of books as from a living and abiding voice.*[8]

In the fourth place, *people learn with greater zest when they intend shortly to teach what they have learned.* This is the experience of schoolteachers and lecturers; it is the experience also of the thousands of un-lettered people who are being brought to literacy through Dr. Frank C. Laubach's methods, adopted by so many colonial governments. To suggest that a man might be a teacher gives him a new self-respect and a new incentive. The early Christian learned that he might teach. No doubt not all proved to be effective teachers. Some exasperation may have lain behind James's expostulation: "Be not many teachers, my brethren" (3:1). There is a sense in which teaching was regarded as a

[7] See *The Thrill of Tradition,* ch. 1.

[8] Eusebius *Historia Ecclesiastica* III. 39.

special gift of the Spirit (see Rom. 12:6-7). Yet ordinary Christians must be "ready always to give answer to every man that asketh you a reason concerning the hope that is in you, yet with meekness and fear: having a good conscience; that, wherein ye are spoken against, they may be put to shame who revile your good manner of life in Christ" (I Peter 3:15-16).

Not all men can be philosophers, nor yet theologians. Nor have all the native wit to fashion the effective reply to a criticism of the faith. There are some things which many must take on trust from those whom they think trustworthy. The effective phrasing of a Spurgeon or a William Temple began its work only when first articulated; it may pass into the speech of large numbers of Christians and go on being used for generations to come. The early Christians trusted the apostles and the men whom they had taught. They came to trust the tradition of teaching which became formulated in the Christian community; they constantly returned to what they had been taught before or after baptism. In the life of the Church the catechism form of question and answer has been found a reliable repository and point of reference for these basic Christian beliefs. A man who has been taught in this way as a child may hear one of the questions many years later, and at once there comes up from his unconsciousness a memory—hazy, perhaps, but sometimes clearly defined—of the answer. It is enough to ask many a Scotsman, "What is the chief end of man?" to bring to his mind an answer which suggests a whole theology: "Man's chief end is to glorify God, and to enjoy him forever." One who has been so instructed, though not himself learned, can at least begin to give answer to every man that asketh him concerning the hope that is in him.

This was a secret which the early Church understood, and a practice which it followed. Dr. Philip Carrington, Archbishop of Quebec, in *The Primitive Christian Catechism,* and Dr. E. G. Selwyn, Dean of Winchester, in his commentary on I Peter, have demonstrated that underlying the epistles were "liturgical and catechetical sources" which were "easily memorized and were composed with that end in view." [9] These might be called "points of crystallization in the common tradition of the Apostolic Church." [10] Whereas at one time it was thought that I Peter was dependent on I Thessalonians —and it is significant that Silvanus had a hand in both letters—it is now thought possible that both writers were drawing on some sort of common pool of tradition.[11] Formulations had been learned by heart from the missionary before he left; when he wrote back to the Church, it was good educational practice to proceed from the known to the unknown, referring to basic lessons already taught, re-emphasizing their importance, and drawing out from them further implications. This happens in missionary work today. Something of the same sort happened in the early Church.

Scholars are thus working at the parallels between the

[9] Selwyn, *op. cit.,* p. 21.
[10] *Ibid.,* p. 19.
[11] *Ibid.,* p. 386.

teaching in the epistles—especially, perhaps, the teaching about baptism—to discover what was common form in a class of catechumens even before our present Gospels were set down in writing. Their reasoning is inevitably complicated, and their evidence too dependent upon parallels in the Greek to be set out here. Yet here is a fruitful new line of New Testament study for the competent scholar. No doubt it will produce its exaggerations as have other new approaches in the past. But it emphasizes afresh our fundamental thesis, that the New Testament is best understood as the literature of a missionary movement. It brings the Church of the New Testament into fresh and living touch with the Church of today, especially the younger churches, but all other churches also which are essaying the perennial missionary task of instructing each generation afresh in the truths of the gospel and the practice of the Christian life.

# X

## *From Speech to Writing*

WHEN the first Christians met together, they talked about Jesus. They came into the fellowship fresh from daily living; and as they discussed the problems it presented, the tasks it set before them, and the decisions which they had continually to be making, the question inevitably arose, What did Jesus do in similar circumstances? Did anyone in the group recall his ever having said anything which bore particularly upon the choice before some one of them? Were they even now meeting a situation about which he had already warned them? If a visitor who was of the Way came from another town, he might be asked, What records have you in your church of Jesus? Have you any stories or sayings of which we are ignorant? Or a man might speak—one who had been in some dusty crowd in Capernaum or Jericho or Jerusalem—saying, "Of his words that I heard there has always been one that stuck in my memory. It's a story about a steward. Does anyone know what it means?"

The first Christians in Jerusalem, says Luke, "continued stedfastly in the apostles' teaching and in fellowship, in the breaking of bread and the prayers" (Acts 2:42). This was the framework of their life, the framework in which their recollections of Jesus arose and, in time, were given a formal shape. From the first they obeyed his command, "This do in remembrance of me." As they met to break the bread and drink the wine, they *remembered* it all again—not just incidents in the Passion Story, but the whole story, moving forward to its triumphant conclusion. The Gospel was spoken at the Eucharist before there was a written Gospel to read. In writing to the churches of Galatia, Paul recalled how Christ was set before them as crucified, "with the clearness of an open proclamation" (3:1) .[1] This must have been true of many Eucharists. There was a story to tell —a story which they could never hear too often, one of death and of life out of death, a story without which their new life and their abounding hope were but a mockery. "If Christ hath not been raised," wrote Paul to the Corinthians, "then is our preaching vain, your faith also is vain" (I Cor. 15:14). The word translated "vain" might perhaps be better rendered "futile."

The story was *told*. At first it was not written. "How shall they hear without a preacher?" (Rom. 10:14) said Paul, not "How shall they read without a scribe?" Frequent reference is made to the word which has been *heard*. "As for you," wrote the author of I John, "let that abide in you which ye heard from the beginning. If that which ye heard from the beginning abide in you, ye shall

[1] B. F. Westcott, *Introduction to the Study of the Gospels* (7th ed.), p. 177.

abide in the Son, and in the Father" (2:24; cf. also vss. 7 and 18, and Eph. 4:20-21). The need for writing was not immediately felt. Their Master had bidden them preach the gospel, not write the gospel. "Christianity was contrasted with Judaism as a dispensation of the Spirit and not of the letter; the laws of which were written not on tables of stone but on the souls of the believers." [2] They did not think of future generations. Were there going to be any? Their Lord was coming again; their task was to prepare, not for posterity, but for his appearing.

Nowadays groups of people sometimes come together, enjoying each other's company, determined to remain quite informal, and not even to keep minutes. Yet circumstances may drive them to appoint a secretary, to enter into correspondence, to keep a record. When a family receives good news, the first impulse of its members is to tell their neighbors all about it; even in the telling the phrases are being formed which they will use in letters that evening. It is only very much later, if at all, that a very careful account of what has taken place comes to be set down in writing. A similar process took place in the life of the early Church. The good news was proclaimed. Very soon letters were being written, but it was a long time before the full accounts in the Gospels were set down. Nevertheless there was an earlier stage, in which a good deal of the material was committed to writing by different hands. Many of these earliest records

[2] *Ibid.*, p. 169.

were not in Greek, the language of the missionary enterprise. They were in Aramaic, the language of the home church.

These writings were probably of three kinds, growing up simultaneously. There were collections of actual sayings of Jesus. That this type of document existed also in the mission field was demonstrated in 1897 by the discovery at Oxyrhynchus, at the edge of the desert 120 miles south of Cairo, of a single papyrus sheet covered on both sides with short sentences beginning "Jesus saith." A second sheet was found in 1903. Some of the sayings on these sheets are familiar from the Gospels, but some are not.

Secondly, there were collections of texts from the Hebrew Scriptures, put together to prove that Jesus was the Messiah. The kind of controversy in which Paul engaged at Thessalonica would require much searching of the Scriptures. Lesser men than Paul might have been glad to have their researches done for them. Few can read the Gospel of Matthew without being struck by the recurrent phrase, "that it might be fulfilled which was spoken by the Lord through the prophet, saying . . ." (cf. Matt. 1:22; 2:15, 17, 18, 23; 4:14; 8:17; 12:17; 13:35; 21:4-5; 27:9). The relevance of the words quoted to the incident they were intended to illustrate was not always very obvious! Matthew's Gospel was written in Greek. One of his sources, however, "must have been a collection of Old Testament prophecies translated with some freedom from the Hebrew, and therefore probably coming originally from Palestinian Christian circles." [3] That he had a list before him is probably made more evident by the fact that Matthew once gave a wrong source for one of these quotations. In 27:9 you may read: "Then was fulfilled that which was spoken by Jeremiah the prophet, saying, And they took thirty pieces of silver," but the reference should be to Zech. 11:13. He had not checked his references! Some sort of commentary must have gone with these proof texts. Perhaps it was oral; perhaps it was written down.

A third type of record would be of actual events. Linguistic students have discovered in some of Mark's sentence construction the kind of grammar which points to an Aramaic original. This may be merely evidence of the type of Greek an Aramaic-speaking Jew would write, but it may be more. "Certainly what evidence we do possess makes the assumption of Aramaic sources for the Marcan narrative much less difficult than for the non-Marcan narrative portions of Matthew and Luke." [4] Luke's Gospel begins in the style of a writer of classical Greek, but the style of the rest of chapter 1 and of chapter 2 is much more reminiscent of the Old Testament, both in the narrative and in the hymns attributed to Mary, Zacharias, and Simeon, which have found so natural a place in the worship of the Church. Here he seems to have been using a source which originally existed in Hebrew or Aramaic. For his record of the speeches of Peter and Stephen he

[3] B. T. D. Smith, *St. Matthew* (Cambridge Greek Testament) , p. xxii.

[4] Matthew Black, *An Aramaic Approach to the Gospels and Acts*, p. 207.

may also have had notes which were originally in Aramaic.

When the first three Gospels are examined together, not only is it made clear that Matthew and Luke used Mark; it is just about as certain that they had another source in common. A comparison will reveal this at once. This is Matt. 3:7-10:

But when he saw many of the Pharisees and Sadducees coming to his baptism, he said unto them, Ye offspring of vipers, who warned you to flee from the wrath to come? Bring forth therefore fruit worthy of repentance: and think not to say within yourselves, We have Abraham to our father: for I say unto you, that God is able of these stones to raise up children unto Abraham. And even now is the axe laid unto the root of the trees: every tree therefore that bringeth not forth good fruit is hewn down, and cast into the fire.

And this is Luke 3:7-9:

He said therefore to the multitudes that went out to be baptized of him, Ye offspring of vipers, who warned you to flee from the wrath to come? Bring forth therefore fruits worthy of repentance, and begin not to say within yourselves, We have Abraham to our father: for I say unto you, that God is able of these stones to raise up children unto Abraham. And even now is the axe laid unto the root of the trees: every tree therefore that bringeth not forth good fruit is hewn down, and cast into the fire.

Here again it is clear that there has been some copying. There are more than two hundred verses of this material which Matthew and Luke have in common, but which is not dependent upon Mark. Scholars are convinced that both had access to a written source—or sources—which has not survived. This material, called Q, cannot, of course, be exactly delimited, because we know only when Matthew and Luke are *both* using it; there are probably places where one draws upon it and the other does not. Yet we know enough about it to describe some of its characteristics.

Q was mainly, though not entirely, made up of teaching. It had almost certainly no narrative of the Passion—it was to supplement that well-known story that this collection of teaching was made. It contained few accounts of Jesus' conflict with the religious leaders. Professor T. W. Manson divides it into four sections: (1) Jesus and John the Baptist; (2) Jesus and his disciples; (3) Jesus and his opponents; (4) sayings about the Last Things. Papias, writing at about A.D. 130, made the enigmatic statement that "Matthew compiled the Logia in the Hebrew language, and everyone translated them as he was able." This can hardly refer to our Gospel of Matthew, which is dependent on Mark, in Greek, and upon Q, which had at least been translated into Greek before the author of Matthew made use of it. It must, however, refer to some book, to some important book, for "Logia," or "Oracles," means sayings of great importance. Apply it to the document Q, says Professor Manson, and this statement "fits like a glove."

Papias said four things: *first,* that a collection of oracles was made; *second,* that it was in Hebrew—by which was meant, as likely as not, the spoken language of

Aramaic; *third,* that it was written by Matthew; and *fourth,* that various people translated it as best they could—doubtless into Greek. Apply this to Q and we find *first* that "Q is a collection of Dominical oracles given for the guidance and encouragement of the new Israel. Just as to the Hebrew saints, whose piety found expression in the Psalter, 'the oracles' meant the commands and promises of God under the Old Covenant, so to the Church 'the oracles' meant the commands and promises of God under the New Covenant." *Second* and *fourth:* a careful examination of the use of Q by Matthew and Luke reveals that while most differences are due to different editorial use, some of them point to the fact that an Aramaic document has been differently translated. "There is a sufficient number of such translation variants to justify the belief that Q was originally an Aramaic document, and that in Matthew and Luke we have two different renderings of it." What of the *third* statement, that it was written by Matthew? There is a presumption in its favor.

When and where was Q written? We can, says Dr. Manson, make only more or less probable conjectures. But: "If it had its origin as a book of instruction for converts from Gentile paganism, it would be natural to connect it with Antioch, the first headquarters of the Gentile mission, and to date it about the middle of the first century, probably rather before than after A.D. 50." [5]

[5] H. D. A. Major, T. W. Manson, and C. J. Wright, *The Mission and Message of Jesus,* p. 312. The quotations in the previous paragraphs are from pp. 310 and 311. The argument depends wholly upon Dr. Manson's

The date is noteworthy. We have made much of the point that the epistles of Paul were written before our Gospels. But now we have pressed back to material underlying two of our Gospels, which may have been written and put into circulation at about the same time as the earliest Pauline epistles, Galatians and Thessalonians.

In the modern Church, when a preacher has a settled ministry, he tries not to repeat himself too much. But a traveling missionary is essentially repetitive. He tells stories over and over again. He finds himself telling them in the same order—indeed a recollection of their order may prevent his having recourse to notes. Those who accompany him on his mission, and any who hear him often, get used to this. They come to expect it; they are disappointed if any familiar touch is omitted, and may well remind him afterward of how he put it last time. (A weary parent, reading a familiar story to a small child, is quickly told if he has skipped a paragraph.) In this way there developed an oral tradition of missionary preaching; and in time around the great centers of Church life, which were all of them missionary headquarters—Jerusalem, Antioch, Caesarea, Rome—a particular way of relating the Christian message became almost standardized. "The primary Gospel was proved, so to speak, in life, before it was fixed in writing," wrote Westcott ninety years ago. "Out of the countless multitude of Christ's acts, those were selected and arranged

-----

work. His section of this valuable book has been published separately by the Student Christian Movement Press under the title of *The Sayings of Jesus.*

during the ministry of twenty years which were seen to have the fullest representative significance for the exhibition of His divine Life. The oral collection thus formed became in every sense coincident with the 'Gospel'; and our Gospels are the permanent compendium of its contents." [6] The modern scholar would not limit the oral period to twenty years; apart from that his position has been very clearly stated.

The missionary work had begun far earlier than this. During his earthly life Jesus sent out the twelve "to preach the kingdom of God, and to heal the sick" (Luke 9:2). The seventy also went out two by two into the cities to "heal the sick that are therein, and say unto them, The kingdom of God is come nigh unto you" (Luke 10:9). They were still ignorant, fallible men. In a sense they had not much to say. But in another sense they had everything to say. They did not speak vaguely about some

> far-off divine event,
> To which the whole creation moves.

The event they proclaimed was divine indeed. They spoke from the excitement of being in the very middle of it. That excitement remained a mark of the early Church.

The Church believed that its Master's last command was to continue the mission into all countries. When Christians were dispersed by the persecution which fol-

---

[6] *Introduction to the Study of the Gospels* (7th ed.), p. 170. The first edition appeared in 1860. This in turn was based upon an earlier book in 1851.

lowed the death of Stephen, the campaign began in earnest. "They therefore that were scattered abroad went about preaching the word. And Philip went down to the city of Samaria, and proclaimed unto them the Christ" (Acts 8:4-5). Here also there was expectation of a Messiah; here too was made the astonishing announcement that he had come, to be rejected and crucified, but to rise from the dead. Philip—like Stephen—was one of the seven who had been appointed deacons, not one of the twelve apostles. He is to reappear in the story.

The Church needed this material. It was needed for teaching catechumens, for reading in worship, for guidance in life, and for the missionary encounters to which every Christian was committed. The parable form which Jesus used served as a kind of literary preservative. Stories were remembered even if their meaning was not understood. Yet how better could the command to love one's neighbor as oneself be made clear than by telling the story of the good Samaritan? (How well this story would have gone in the original mission in Samaria! Was it Philip who recounted it later on to Luke? That is at least possible.) When a young preacher met failure, one can imagine one of the apostles saying to him: "The Master met failure too—a great deal of it. At first, of course, it looked as if everything was going well; we half imagined that there'd be a march on Jerusalem! But then the opposition started—and we were wrong anyway. But Jesus told a story just then—about the kinds of soil on which our message is sown. I think it about fits your case. It goes like this. . . ."

Practical guidance was needed on questions of daily importance. What attitude should be taken toward paying taxes and toward divorce? At once the teaching of Jesus on these matters would be recalled by those who knew it. We know that Paul was sometimes asked, Is there a word of the Lord on this matter? (I Cor. 7:10, 12.) Other missionaries must have been asked similar questions. Arguments were also required which could be used against opponents, both Gentile and Jewish. For the latter the stories of our Lord's encounters with the Pharisees woud be invaluable—for example, Mark 2:13-28; 7:19; and the whole of chapter 12. Lastly there was the Passion Story, told in far greater completeness and with far more constant repetition.

In Acts 24:27 we learn that Paul was imprisoned in Caesarea for two full years after his arrest in Jerusalem, and before his voyage to Rome. During this time—around A.D. 57-59—Luke was with him. The principal people in the church at Caesarea were Philip and his family, with whom the missionaries had stayed earlier (Acts 21:8-9). How did Luke spend his time? Many scholars believe that he was making the researches which lie behind his Gospel, and was preparing its first draft. What had he to go upon? There was the missionary preaching which he had so often heard and in which he had taken part; he had not shepherded the young church at Philippi for nothing. The document was already in circulation. And he had many opportunities in Caesarea and its neighborhood to question those who had been with Jesus. When he set to work, he found that there was much literary material for him to use; some of its most precious parts have come down to us from him alone. Luke, as we have it, contains much of Mark; and it used to be held that this was before him as he wrote his Gospel at the first. His use of Mark, however, is different from that of Matthew. He puts whole sections of it in and leaves much out. Some scholars think this was because he was fitting it into a document which had already been written. This theory of a Proto-Luke is at least possible, and it is more than likely that Luke was beginning collecting his material when he was at Caesarea, if not earlier. His own preface serves as a summary of all the work which had been already done before the Gospels we know were written. Here he makes the claim to be a careful historian. He was not himself an eyewitness, but he had paid scrupulous attention to the accounts of those who were. Dr. Moffatt's translation says:

Inasmuch as a number of writers have essayed to draw up a narrative of the established facts in our religion, exactly as these have been handed down to us by the original eyewitnesses who were in the service of the Gospel Message, and inasmuch as I have gone carefully over them all from the beginning, I have decided, O Theophilus, to write them out in order for your excellency, to let you know the solid truth of what you have been taught. (Luke 1:1-4.)

The book is thus dedicated to an official who may be addressed as "Your Excellency." His name, Theophilus, which means a lover of God, may have been a pseudonym to conceal the identity of some figure in public life whose interest in the Christian religion had not yet been made public. When Luke wrote his second volume—the Acts of the Apostles—he dedicated it also to Theophilus. But this time he is no longer called "Your Excellency." It is tempting to imagine that the earlier instruction in the solid truth had brought him well within a community where titles of honor did not matter very much.

# XI

## The Four Gospels

THE word "gospel" has been used in two senses in this book: first for the good news preached by the original apostles and their successors; second for the four short written books, unique in the literature of the world, in which that good news is set out in fuller detail. The use of the word to describe one of these books—which in the Greek New Testament are only headed "According to Matthew," and so on—is probably derived from the opening verse of Mark: "The beginning of the gospel of Jesus Christ, the Son of God." The words "the Son of God" are not in all the manuscripts, but textual criticism tends to retain rather than reject them. As they stand, they are a complete answer to those people who want to "get behind theology to the simple gospel," for this opening of the briefest of the Gospels is packed with theology. There is a sense in which the gospel *is* simple—but it is God's simplicity and not man's. It is not a vague story about a preacher of goodness who was misunderstood and put to death. The written Gospels tell the same story as the verbal preaching, a story of God in action at history's greatest crisis. The good news was, at least, that the Messiah had come. Mark goes on to tell what his coming meant; and it is not very long before he records how men said: "Why doth this man thus speak? he blasphemeth: who can forgive sins but one, even God" (2:7).

This Gospel, which was used as we have seen by Matthew and Luke, was almost certainly written for the church in Rome shortly after the Neronian persecution in A.D. 64, in which both Peter and Paul were put to death. "And after their deaths," wrote Irenaeus in about A.D. 180, "Mark, the disciple and interpreter of Peter, himself also handed down to us in writing the things which Peter had proclaimed." If this is true, it is very important. For it means that in Mark we have at least a fragmentary indication of Peter's preaching. May not Peter have begun a sermon roughly as follows? "How well I remember those early days. It was just after John the Baptist had been put into prison. Jesus came into Galilee, preaching the gospel of God, and saying, The time is fulfilled and the kingdom of God is at hand: repent ye and believe in the gospel" (Mark 1:14-15). Here, at any rate, we have a remarkable summary of the missionary preaching of the early Church. It may have been Peter who recalled that "there was no longer room for them, no, not even about the door," yet that in the melee of that house in Capernaum "there were certain of the scribes *sitting* there" (Mark 2:2, 6). There are many such touches in Mark which suggest the recollections of an eyewitness, touches removed by the skillful précis-writing of Matthew and in the fitting together of different sources at which Luke was equally skilled.

Is this tradition to be trusted? There are earlier evidences of it than Irenaeus. A little before his date what are called the Anti-Marcionite Prologues to the Gospels stated that: "Mark, who was called stump-fingered because his fingers were small by comparison with the rest of his body, was Peter's interpreter, and after Peter's decease wrote down this same Gospel in the region of Italy." Perhaps at about A.D. 130 is the testimony of Papias: "Mark, having become the interpreter of Peter, wrote down accurately everything that he remembered, without however recording in order what was said or done by Christ." So much for external evidence. Is it supported by the New Testament itself?

There are eight references in the New Testament to one who bears the name of John Mark. Let us track them down. The first is in Acts 12:12, where Peter, miraculously released from prison in Jerusalem, "came to the house of Mary the mother of John whose surname was Mark; where many were gathered together and were praying." This tells us (1) that Mark was a young man, as his mother is named as the owner of the house; (2) that it was a large house; (3) that it was the place to which Peter naturally turned, expecting to find the church assembled. In Acts 12:25 Barnabas and Paul leave for Antioch to begin what proves to be Paul's first missionary journey, and they take John Mark with them. In Acts 13:13 before the high Taurus Mountains the young man leaves the party and makes tracks for home. The next reference is Acts 15:37-39. Plans are made for a second missionary journey. Barnabas suggests Mark as a suitable companion. Paul replies, "Not at any price. Have you forgotten how he left us last time?" Yet for some reason not immediately apparent Barnabas took Mark's side so strongly that he separated from Paul and went off with Mark to Cyprus.

The next reference, Col. 4:10, comes a good deal later. Paul is writing from prison, probably in Rome. Mark is with him; and we begin to understand why Barnabas previously championed him so vigorously, for he is here described as "the cousin of Barnabas," which may mean that he was his nephew. The reconciliation with Paul appears complete. The Colossians are told to give him a proper reception. In the personal letter written at the same time to Philemon, Paul describes Mark as a fellow worker. In II Tim. 4:11 he is described as useful for ministering. Lastly there is a reference in I Pet. 5:13. Peter writing from "Babylon," which is an unpleasant way of saying Rome, speaks of "Mark my son," which is a pleasant way of expressing affection for a pupil.

Mark was not, therefore, a witness of the whole ministry of Jesus; but he was closely associated with Paul and Peter, and had done a missionary journey with Barnabas as well, to whom he was closely related. At his home in Jerusalem the church used to meet in the early days. Was this the house in which the Last Supper took place? That is likely. And was Mark the man carrying the pitcher of water (Mark 14:13) who guided the disciples to the house? That also is likely. If so, it provides an explanation for a little passage in the Passion narrative which occurs in Mark and nowhere else: "And a certain young man followed with him, having a linen cloth cast about him, over his naked body: and they lay hold on him; but he left the linen cloth, and fled naked" (14:51-52). Why is this odd incident recounted—unless Mark was himself the young man in question who slipped out in his night clothes after the party had left the house, to see what was happening? The temple guards got his dressing gown—but they did not get him. This also would serve as a reply to stories which might well have been going the rounds about Mark's cowardice in turning back at the foot of the Taurus Mountains; for the story follows the sentence: "And they all left him, and fled." When that happened, there was still one young man who followed. It is more important to remember that the presence of the young man near the Garden of Gethsemane might explain how the words spoken there by Jesus—when the three chosen disciples were overcome by fatigue—came to be reported.

Mark's narrative is a graphic one, moving swiftly toward its climax. He was not a great writer, but he had a great story to tell. His outline was followed, in the main, by Matthew and Luke. Nowadays scholars are asking, Is that outline in any way reliable? Did not Mark just string together the stories already current in the oral tradition, adding one to another where it seemed to fit best, but with no tradition of a chronological kind to guide him? Did not even Papias say that he did not set out the events in order? Some of the form critics thus deny the reliability of the outline. Yet, as Professor Dodd has put it, these questions must be asked:

Was there, or was there not a point in the life of Jesus at which He summoned His followers to accompany Him to Jerusalem with the prospect of suffering and death? Is it, or it is not likely that from that point on His thought and His speech dwelt with special emphasis upon the theme of His approaching Passion? [1]

Say yes to the questions, and Mark's Gospel, which is found upon examination to contain all the main points in the early Christian preaching, reveals itself as no mere stringing together of stories. It represents rather "a genuine succession of events within which movement and development can be traced." [2]

If Mark is the interpreter of Peter, it is interesting to note that he makes no attempt to evade Peter's weaknesses. For his readers, however, the situation would have been transfigured by Peter's martyrdom. "To start with he had many of our weaknesses," we can imagine them saying, "but in the end he gave his life an offering to God." This would further encourage them for trials which might lie ahead, and it is a clue to Mark's Gospel to remember that it was written for a martyr church.

At Luke's Gospel we have already looked. We have seen the possibility of its having existed in two forms, the first having been prepared before Mark came his

[1] *The Expository Times,* XLII (1932) , 397.
[2] *Ibid.,* p. 400.

way. Proto-Luke was then enlarged by the insertion at suitable points of blocks of Marcan material. This, as Professor Vincent Taylor has pointed out, "is not an imaginative account of the composition of Luke forced on the text, but an attempt to explain a complicated series of facts within the Gospel itself." [3] Yet whether we accept this account or not, Luke's sources are fairly evident. There was—sooner or later—Mark. There was also Q. There were a number of special sources to which he alone among the evangelists had access. These may have been partly gathered at Caesarea. The birth stories, with their markedly Hebraic character, are distinct among these; and some who hold the Proto-Luke theory believe that they also, like Mark, were added later.

Recent discoveries have vindicated Luke's accuracy as a historian at one particular point. In 2:2-3 he wrote: "This was the first enrolment made when Quirinius was governor of Syria. And all went to enrol themselves, every one to his own city." Here, it used to be held, there were three mistakes: there was no such census; Quirinius was not governor of Syria at the time; people did not go to their ancestral homes to be enrolled when a census did take place. Census papers have, however, been found in the papyri in Egypt which lead to the belief that they took place every fourteen years. We know that there was one in A.D. 6. A census paper has been recovered for A.D. 34, and probably one for A.D. 20. We can at least make a conjecture that one took place

[3] *The Gospels,* p. 36. Ch. 5 in this book is the best short exposition of the theory.

around 8 B.C. Quirinius came to Syria in A.D. 6, and he was in charge of the census then. A stone has been found which shows that he was in Syria also in 6 B.C. Some think that the census of 8 B.C. was delayed in Judaea until 6 B.C.—and this is held to be a more likely date for the birth of Jesus than the traditional one. Did people go to their ancestral homes for a census? A few pages from a Roman official's letter book dated A.D. 104 have been found at Oxyrhynchus—and they contain an instruction to the prefect of Egypt ordering all people to go back to the county in which they live within the next six weeks in order to be ready for the census.

The characteristics of Luke's Gospel have often been enumerated. Readers should note his widespread sympathies, international and social, as we might call them today. His has been called the Gospel of the underdog. It is a Gospel in which there is a special emphasis on prayer, and in which a special sympathy is shown toward women. The birth stories—which may even come from the Virgin Mary herself—are certainly written from a woman's point of view. Yet there is also a note of sternness in the sayings of Jesus, more marked here than perhaps anywhere else. The theme of the Passion dominates the story. The Gospel is not halfway through before we read: "He stedfastly set his face to go to Jerusalem" (9:51). It is, interestingly enough, a Hebraic phrase. The story from that point becomes a pilgrimage to the Cross.

Mark's Gospel is usually dated at about A.D. 65, Luke's at about A.D. 80, and Matthew's a little later. There are indications of a late date in the text itself. Thus Matt. 27:8 suggests the perspective of a later period, "Wherefore that field was called, The field of blood, unto this day," as does also 28:15, "And this saying was spread abroad among the Jews, and continueth until this day." It should not disturb us that the Gospel cannot nowadays be attributed to Matthew himself, though we have seen the possibility that he might be the author of Q. After all, when it was first quoted by Ignatius and other writers, it was simply called "The Gospel"; and the familiar title was no part of the original text. Written in Greek, and dependent upon Greek sources, it is yet the most Jewish of the Gospels. It must have been written for a Jewish Church in a bilingual area. Not only does it emphasize the fulfillment of prophecy. Its teaching material is gathered together in five books, an arrangement which seems to be a conscious reflection of the five books of the Jewish Law. If the reader will look up 7:28-29; 11:1; 13:53; 19:1; and 26:1, he will discover the recurring formula—"and it came to pass, when Jesus had finished all these words, he . . ."—which concludes each of these books. It is to be noted also that each concludes, not only with a formula, but "with a pointed allusion to the rewards and punishments of the Day of Judgment. In this respect Matthew has justly been described as the most apocalytic of the Gospels." [4]

The first of these books is familiar as the Sermon on the Mount, a title customary in English translations

[4] F. W. Green, *The Gospel According to St. Matthew*, Clarendon Bible, p. 8.

since the Great Bible, ordered to be set up in churches in 1540, which spoke of "the most excellent and lovynge sermon of Chryst in the Mount: which sermon is the very keye that openeth the understanding into the lawe." The annotator here has caught the vision of the evangelist, that of the new Lawgiver proclaiming the new Law to the new Israel from the new Sinai. The question naturally arises, Did anything of this kind really take place? Granted that the teaching goes back to Jesus, has it not just been collected together by Matthew for the sake of impressiveness and convenience?

If this were entirely true, it would not, perhaps, matter very much. We have already conceded that Matthew did group his teaching material in this way. Some of the teaching in the Sermon on the Mount may be found elsewhere in Luke. He has, however, a similar though much shorter sermon, given "on a level place" (Luke 6:17, 20-49). (B. H. Streeter held that Luke gave the Q version of the sermon, and that Matthew conflated this with a special source of his own.[5] This would account for the difference in the Beatitudes.) Both Matthew and Luke link it with the call of the disciples, putting it after the earlier proclamation of the Kingdom of God. Mark has no sermon, but the Marcan order helps to recover what may have taken place. In Mark 3:13-14 the choice of the disciples, on a mountain, comes at a significant point. The proclamation of the Kingdom of God in 1:14-15 has been followed by acts of healing and by widespread popularity, "insomuch that Jesus could no

[5] *The Four Gospels*, p. 251.

more openly enter into a city, but was without in desert places: and they came to him from every quarter" (1:45). Widespread popularity is followed by intense, if limited, unpopularity. The charges mount against him. He blasphemes (2:7); he mixes with the wrong people (2:16); he is not serious enough (2:18); he breaks our rules (2:24); he is too dangerous to be permitted (3:6). This leads to the alliance with the Herodians, which Burkitt described as almost a complaint to the police. We can imagine the religious leaders saying: "It takes a lot to bring us to have any dealings with you. But the situation is serious indeed. You have already dealt with John the Baptist. There is a man going round now who is ten times more dangerous than he was."

At this point, says Mark, "Jesus with his disciples withdrew to the sea" (3:7) —and the word "withdrew" may have meant much more of a tactical withdrawal than has usually been supposed. His campaign would now demand *cohesion* both in personnel and in principles. He would need to know those who were really on his side. They would need to know more clearly what he actually stood for. The two needs would be met by the choice of twelve disciples from the wider group— after a night of prayer, as Luke characteristically reminds us—and by a fuller and more sustained teaching discourse than they had yet heard. This teaching was given to the disciples in the hearing of the multitudes. It is not an appeal to conversion but an indication of what conversion implies. Some from the multitude who heard the teaching might well want to know more about it and that mysterious coming of the Kingdom of God upon which it was all based.

For the author of Matthew, Mark's Gospel was no new discovery to be fitted into an existing framework. He was a man who knew Mark almost by heart, hence his freedom in rewriting. Yet he was writing at a time when it was no longer considered reverent to treat the central figure in the story—or even the subsidiary figures—with Mark's freedom. Mark wrote of Jesus' return to Nazareth: "And he could do there no mighty work" (6:5) because of their unbelief. Matthew tones it down to "he did not many mighty works there because of their unbelief" (13:58). There are other similiar instances in both Matthew and Luke, indicative of a later date. Matthew's Gospel reveals the reverence of the Church for its Master. Its use in worship swiftly became general, almost to eclipse all others. Its author must have been more of a pastor than an evangelist. Perhaps he has unconsciously provided a self-portrait in 13:52: "Every scribe who hath been made a disciple to the kingdom of heaven is like unto a man that is a house-holder, which bringeth forth out of his treasure things new and old."

John's Gospel is certainly the work of one who has been a missionary. The echoes of that controversy which was a necessity for the establishment of the Church among both Jews and Gentiles sound through its pages, adding sometimes, we believe, a sharper note to the remembered words of Jesus. In no other Gospel is the missionary purpose so explicit. "These are written, that ye may believe that Jesus is the Christ, the Son of God; and that believing ye may have life in his name." (20:31.) Yet the Gospel was also written to meet a particular situation in the Church where it was to be read. Its author was concerned to root out heresy of a kind which might imperil the future of the faith.

The modern heretic is usually one who denies the divinity of Jesus. The earliest heretics denied his humanity. We have already read the plain words of the Johannine epistles, renouncing as "the deceiver and antichrist" those who denied that Jesus Christ came in the flesh.[6] Augustine "put his finger upon the point when he said that most of the statements made in the Prologue to the Fourth Gospel were already familiar to him from the writings of the Neo-Platonists; but one thing he could not find there: 'The Word was made flesh.' "[7] The key to the Fourth Gospel has at times been found in the popular philosophy of the Hellenistic world and in the works of Philo, the Alexandrian Jew contemporary with Jesus, who strove so valiantly to effect a reconciliation between Jewish religion and Greek philosophy—"but," asks Hoskyns, "and the question is important, did the poor and the ignorant, when they lay a-dying, ever ask their Rabbis to read to them out of the voluminous writings of Philo, or of those like

[6] Cf. p. 126.

[7] C. H. Dodd, *The Johannine Epistles,* "Moffatt New Testament Commentary," p. xxi. The reference is to the *Confessions* VII. 9.

him?" [8] For nine out of ten Christians the Fourth Gospel is the most prized book in the Bible.

We have other evidence to show it was written earlier than was at one time supposed. In the Rylands Library at Manchester, England, is a tiny scrap of papyrus which is the oldest known fragment of the New Testament—and it is a fragment of John! The experts in papyrology conclude of this actual scrap of writing that "one can hardly go wrong in dating it in the first half of the second century." [9] Early tradition was sure that this Gospel was written in Ephesus. From Asia Minor to Middle Egypt, where this fragment was found, is a long way. It may have taken thirty years or more to have got there. This supports the belief of those who hold that the Fourth Gospel was written no later than the turn of the first century.

The critical reader, turning from the Synoptic Gospels to John, finds himself in a new world. Where are the familiar parables? Why is it that the short epigrammatic teaching has been displaced by lengthy discourses? How is it that there is no proclamation of the Kingdom of God, but instead teaching about eternal life? How is it that the miracles which the Synoptic Jesus was so reluctant to perform have here become signs—which the Synoptic Jesus refused to give? In the Synoptic Gospels, Jesus is not recognized as the Messiah until fairly late in his ministry; in the Fourth Gospel this recognition

[8] *The Fourth Gospel* (rev. ed.), p. 20.

[9] Sir Frederick Kenyon, quoted in C. H. Roberts, *An Unpublished Fragment of the Fourth Gospel,* p. 15.

comes in the first chapter. Furthermore the whole style of writing is different. Speech and comment fade into each other so that it is often hard to tell which is which. When Jesus speaks, it is in the style of the author of the Johannine epistles. In the Synoptic Gospels the ministry centers upon Galilee; Jesus does not reach the capital until the last week. In John the ministry centers largely around the succession of feasts in Jerusalem. Much of the teaching is given in the temple itself; location and language seem constantly pointing to Old Testament prophecies which speak of the Lord's voice going forth from Jerusalem.[10] Again and again it becomes obvious that there is more in the narrative than meets the outward eye.

Yet there are indications in the Synoptic tradition that Jesus knew the capital and its environs well. Arrangements were made in advance with the owner of the unbroken ass, to be ridden first by Jesus in his triumphal entry (Mark 11:1-10). Jesus was well known in Bethany (Mark 11:11). Foresight entered into the plans for the house in which the Last Supper was to be held (Mark 14:13-16). And do we not remember his lamentation over the city? "O Jerusalem, Jerusalem, which killeth the prophets, and stoneth them that are sent unto her! how often would I have gathered thy children together, even as a hen gathereth her own brood under her wings, and ye would not." (Luke 13:34; cf. Matt. 23:37, also Luke 13:33.) [11] This would lose most of its

[10] Cf. Hoskyns, *op. cit.*, p. 64.
[11] The saying is from Q.

point if Jesus had not even been to the city since he was twelve.

In addition to this the Q document contains one saying which is surprisingly Johannine in language:

At that season Jesus answered and said, I thank thee, O Father, Lord of heaven and earth, that thou didst hide these things from the wise and understanding, and didst reveal them unto babes: yea, Father, for so it was well-pleasing in thy sight. All things have been delivered unto me of my Father: and no one knoweth the Son, save the Father; neither doth any know the Father, save the Son, and he to whomsoever the Son willeth to reveal him. (Matthew 11:25-27; cf. Luke 10:21-22.)

Is this an intrusion of Hellenism into the primitive Christian tradition? Quite the reverse. The passage, when translated into Aramaic, is found to be poetry. It is "full of Semitic turns of phrase, and certainly Palestinian in origin. There is no good reason for doubting its authenticity." [12]

This saying gives a key to what has happened in the Fourth Gospel. A part of the original tradition has become the basis of a Johannine discourse. Upon examination it is found that this has happened again and again. It is assumed that the readers of the Fourth Gospel know the Synoptic tradition. They have a miscellaneous amount of information from which they may well be inclined to pick and choose. The Fourth Gospel reorders

[12] Manson, *op. cit.*, p. 371. The *Fragments of an Unknown Gospel*, edited for the British Museum in 1935, also have marked Johannine characteristics.

it for them. Here there can be no picking and choosing; it is one consistent portrait that is being painted. The theme is "set forth with so great an economy of language that very few words suffice to define it. *Father, Son, Life, Light, Love, Truth, Judgment, believing, knowing, seeing*—by means of these words the theme of the Gospel is fully defined." [13] It is a theological theme; yet its basis is found to consist in words, sayings, incidents, already familiar to us and to the book's first readers, from the Synoptic tradition. We know what the book is about because we have already read the Synoptists.

Can we go further and say that we know what the Synoptists were after because we have read John? That was the conclusion of Scott Holland:

The primary effect of the Synoptic Gospels may be direct and simple; but, as soon as our attention has got to work upon them, we see that, far from being self-sufficient and complete, they offer no explanation whatever of the presentation which they offer us. They give no account of themselves. They raise problems for which they offer no solution. They provoke questions which they never attempt to answer. They leave off at a point where it is impossible to stop. [14]

Not only was the Fourth Gospel needed for devotion. It was needed, in some ways, to correct the Synoptic tradition. It was needed as a basis for Christian thinking.

[13] Hoskyns, *op. cit.*, pp. 68-69.
[14] *The Fourth Gospel*, pp. 1-2.

The Synoptic Jesus claims to forgive sins, and the religious leaders are naturally scandalized. But the disciples accept this claim. The Johannine record gives it an understandable basis.

This work comes at the end of the apostolic age—indeed it could hardly have come before. It meets men's needs, answers their questions, and brings them afresh to worship. At a time when the missionary faith of Christianity was in danger of being watered down into a generalized theosophy there comes the ringing answer of the Word made flesh. The Fourth Gospel, says Professor Dodd, can best be understood as a brilliant attempt to undercut this whole process "by a genuine and thoroughgoing reinterpretation, in which alien categories are completely mastered and transformed by the Gospel and constrained to express the central truth of Christianity in universal terms." [15] The Greek world wanted Jesus at its own price, as a spiritual influence only and not as one who had taken on flesh and blood. It was only through being lifted up from the earth, in the bitter anguish of crucifixion, that he began the process in which history finds its meaning and consummation, of drawing all men to himself.

[15] *The Johannine Epistles,* pp. xvii-xviii.

# *Index of Scripture References*

## OLD TESTAMENT

## NEW TESTAMENT

# Index of Subjects

*173*